Ghosts of Waukesha

Josh Hughes
with R. Michael Huberty

**AMERICAN
GHOST BOOKS**

Cover illustrations by Anna Huffman
Printed in the United States of America
ISBN 979-8-9915482-7-4

CONTENTS

INTRODUCTION:
THE GHOSTS OF WAUKESHA

It's safe to say I think about ghosts more on a daily basis than I bet your average person does in their entire life. It all started as a curiosity when I experienced unexplainable things in my childhood home. Since then, it has blossomed into an instinct. Either I'm drawn to haunted locations or spirits are attracted to me; I'm unsure which is more unsettling. My journey as a paranormal investigator rightfully has its own chapter but the most important part is that it all started right here in Waukesha.

Since becoming the Waukesha Ghost Walks tour guide in 2021, Waukesha's haunted and bizarre history has been my sole focus. While I have an interest in Wisconsin and beyond, I take great pride in being the expert on all things Fortean right here in Waukesha. However, there's one question that left me drawing a blank and has been driving my research ever since.

My third season as a tour guide, I really started to become more confident in my abilities to effectively tell a ghost story. The notecards I referenced stayed tucked in my pants pocket longer, I knew more about the places and people involved with the stories, and I even started to gather my own personal experiences by visiting some of the haunted locations. However, it was this summer that one of the guests asked me one of the simplest yet compelling questions I've ever been asked.

"How long does a haunting last?"

I was like a deer caught in the headlights. Somehow the idea that a haunting could cease to exist is not a thought that's ever crossed my mind. The guest probably didn't expect me to have an existential crisis over this but it left enough of an impression to begin the journey I'm about to take you on.

"When does a ghost expire?"

"Do they ever go away?"

These questions are as complex to answer as, "What happens when we die?"

Many people believe when we die, the only thing that remains is our spirit. This is the energy that becomes a ghost, in theory. Just like death, there are many theories that put an expiration date on spirits. After so many years the energy is so diminished that it simply ceases to exist. But that certainly wouldn't explain why some castles in Ireland are still haunted thousands of years later. In that regard it might not be the strength of our energy but in fact the location that determines how long our spirit will remain. Regardless it's comforting to know that when we die, there is still a part of us that could exist forever on earth. Theoretically speaking, of course.

Whether spirits remain and choose to engage with us or not, their stories still live on. Knowing the story gives us more focus on interacting with a potentially haunted location. I find the more information we can arm ourselves with, the better the outcome. Just think if you had a random person walking into your house and asking what your name is you'd be a bit caught off guard too. Instead by learning the history, names, ages, and events that took place in a location, we can fit in much better. Much like learning a foreign language while traveling to a new land.

In these last five years as the self-appointed "Waukesha Ghost Expert," I've taken it upon myself to not only tell historically accurate stories, but to visit and investigate many of the locations myself. Knowing the history and the ghostly legends has led me to encounter some pretty remarkable things. While interacting with the spirit of Les Paul certainly wasn't on my bucket list, it's a fun story to tell the grandkids one day. Even with my headstrong attitude to debunk evidence of the supernatural, I can confidently say that many of the locations are genuinely haunted.

Some of them are also not haunted and remain a good ghost story to share with friends. While it is disappointing when you can disprove a story, it's still fun to share that journey. Research isn't easy and it can lead you down a lot of rabbit holes that end up nowhere. But to provide the most authentic and historically accurate tour possible, sometimes you're going to end up finding things that prove your ghost stories false. While there is only one story I tell that ends up being a fraud, it's important to point those things out to make a point that there's nothing worse than a fake ghost story.

With that being said, the stories you are about to read are a wonderful blend of Waukesha history, lore, and first-hand encounters from my point of view. A unique twist that makes it a tale only I can tell. This journey will take you to historic cemeteries, a cursed farm, Wisconsin's oldest college, and my current home with a spirit as friendly as Casper residing here. Every encounter and first visit is as exciting and terrifying as the last. Whether there is tragic loss or friendly spirits, it still sends a shiver up my spine.

Most of the time I tend to seek out a haunted location, sheepishly asking the property owner if they know about the ghost story. However, it's not uncommon for word to get around and the owner reaches out to me. While that is a rare occurrence, it leads to some of the most fascinating visits where I've discovered what I know and what I've researched has only scratched the surface. There's something to say about going above and beyond to dive deep into the lore of this history. While the fruit isn't always worth the squeeze, the few times you get more than you bargained for make it end up being worthwhile. In these interactions I have learned the ghost exists whether people know the story or whether they choose to believe in it or not.

Please read the following with an open mind and a thirst for knowledge.

A BRIEF HISTORY OF WAUKESHA

Looking back just 200 years, Waukesha was drastically different than it is today. Like much of Wisconsin, Waukesha is influenced heavily by the Native American culture that was here long before us. The primary Native American tribe associated with the Waukesha area is the Potawatomi. In fact, the name "Waukesha" itself is believed to be derived from a Potawatomi word meaning "fox." Other tribes that may have occupied the region include the Menominee, Ojibwe (Chippewa), and Ho-Chunk (Winnebago). However, when the first white settlers arrived, much of the native population were forced to relinquish their land through treaties and were removed from the area by the 1830s.

The Potawatomi were around long enough to meet one of Waukesha's first white settlers, Morris Cutler. Since there is a ghost story associated with his tale, we'll save his story for later. At that time Waukesha was known as Prairieville, eventually adopting the name Waukesha in 1847. As Waukesha grew in population, it attracted people from across the United States. One of those people had a life altering event that put the city on the map for more than 45 years.

It was a hot August day in the summer of 1868 when Colonel Richard Dunbar of New York was in Waukesha visiting his sister-in-law. The last few years had been rough, as Dunbar was severely weakened by diabetes. Perpetually thirsty and exhausted, he rested under an oak tree in what is now known as Bethesda Park. The only comfort he could find was drinking water from the nearby spring. At first it was a few glasses, then a few more, then as much as six glasses of fresh spring water a day. Anytime he's drinking water he

5

feels better and whenever he isn't, constant suffering. Within months, his diabetes was completely cured.

Colonel Richard Dunbar. Photo: Waukesha County Historical Society & Museum

With Dunbar's entrepreneurial spirit, much to the citizens of Waukesha's dismay, he turned the Bethesda Spring into a fountain of wealth. By the time Dunbar died just nine years later, he had already turned Waukesha into the Springs City. Bethesda Spring

---

[1] Colonel Richard Dunbar. Photo: Waukesha County Historical Society & Museum

was one of 60 springs in the city. Many of them attracted visitors from across the world looking to cure all sorts of ailments of their own. Hygeia Spring at one point was on the verge of supplying the World's Fair in Chicago with fresh spring water from Waukesha. Many of the citizens opposed the idea and eventually ran the businessman responsible out of town.

While most citizens weren't fond of the tourist attraction Waukesha would become, many others saw the financial opportunities the magical healing water brought to the city. With the Spring's Era, Waukesha became a resort town. Dozens of hotels popped up across the city, giving room and board to the 25 trainloads of people that came to our city every day. Many of those hotels no longer exist except for a very few that we'll get to later.

Eventually, the Springs Era ran dry. Today, there are only a handful of actual springs that still exist with only one of them having

---

[2] Bethesda Springs. Photo: Waukesha County Historical Society & Museum

drinkable water. If you take a trip to Frame Park, you'll find Hobo Springs between the park and Formal Gardens. While the water looks crystal clear and quite refreshing on a hot summer's day, you do not want to drink it.

For years, the famous tree Dunbar sat under was one of the only remaining glimpses back into the Springs Era, but it too would suffer a fateful ending. In 1991, a thunderstorm ripped through Waukesha and the Dunbar Oak was struck by lightning, obliterating it. Growing up on Dunbar Avenue, just a short walk from Bethesda Park, visiting the remains of the Dunbar Oak after the storm was one of my first memories as a toddler. I remember the mighty tree completely split open and the orange-ish wood on the inside spilling out in a visceral mess.

---

[3] Hobo Spring. Photo: Josh Hughes

This is one of the only events your author was able to experience first-hand. The rest of my personal experiences with these stories and locations are happening decades, if not a century, after the events occurred. While a story is good to hear, I believe it becomes a great story when you're able to walk the same path as those who experienced it. It almost feels like you're able to step right back in time, feeling and seeing the same things these people once saw in their day-to-day lives.

---

[4] The Author's Family at The Dunbar Oak. Photo: Josh Hughes

CLUB 400

Whether it's well-deserved or self-appointed, Club 400 has always been known as "world famous." The charming two-story brick building on Williams Street has had quite the reputation across Waukesha for some time now. From its heyday as a hotel, to the grand opening of its current name, to the many homecoming celebrations for Carroll University, Club 400 is a place of memories throughout the generations. Some of those memories seem to remain deep within the walls, as strange occurrences comfort and plague past and current owners. Perhaps "a curse of sorts" leading back to the very first owner of the establishment once known as The Northwestern Hotel.

Club 400, built in 1894, sits opposite the former Chicago and Northwestern Depot. Originally owned by Valentine Imig, it served as a restaurant and hotel for passengers who got off daily at the train station next door. There is an overwhelming belief, although not proven, that tunnels ran underneath Williams Street between the hotel and the nearby Fox Head Brewery that allowed for transporting beer kegs to the bar.

The centuries old lore surrounding this building might very well lie with a discovery Imig made on the property. His former residence was at one time right next to the hotel where the current parking lot is located. Imig was digging in the backyard when he unearthed human remains he believed were that of a Native American. After this incident, nothing but bad luck seemed to plague Imig and his family. He met his untimely demise in an automobile accident just east of the city on September 12, 1914. His funeral was held at his home on Williams Street. After Imig, the building had numerous owners and uses over the years. Once prohibition hit, it was an ice cream store and cigar shop. Eventually in 1948, George and Ralph Polsfuss purchased the building and renamed it Club 400 after the Chicago Northwestern Railroad that would stop across the street every day at 4 p.m. George and Ralph just happened to be the father and brother of Waukesha's most famous son, Les Paul, so of course they got him to play at the grand opening of the new night club on Williams Street.

The Wizard of Waukesha, Les Paul, was born in 1915 just as the Springs Era was coming to a close. Experimenting with instruments from a young age, it was as early as 1928 that Les was already coming up with ways to make his acoustic guitar louder. A drive for big sound that would eventually lead him to create the very first electric guitar. As his fame grew and he was traveling all across the world, Les still made frequent trips back to Waukesha where he'd always seem to find his way back to Club 400 to visit family.

[5] Inside Club 400. Photo: Club 400

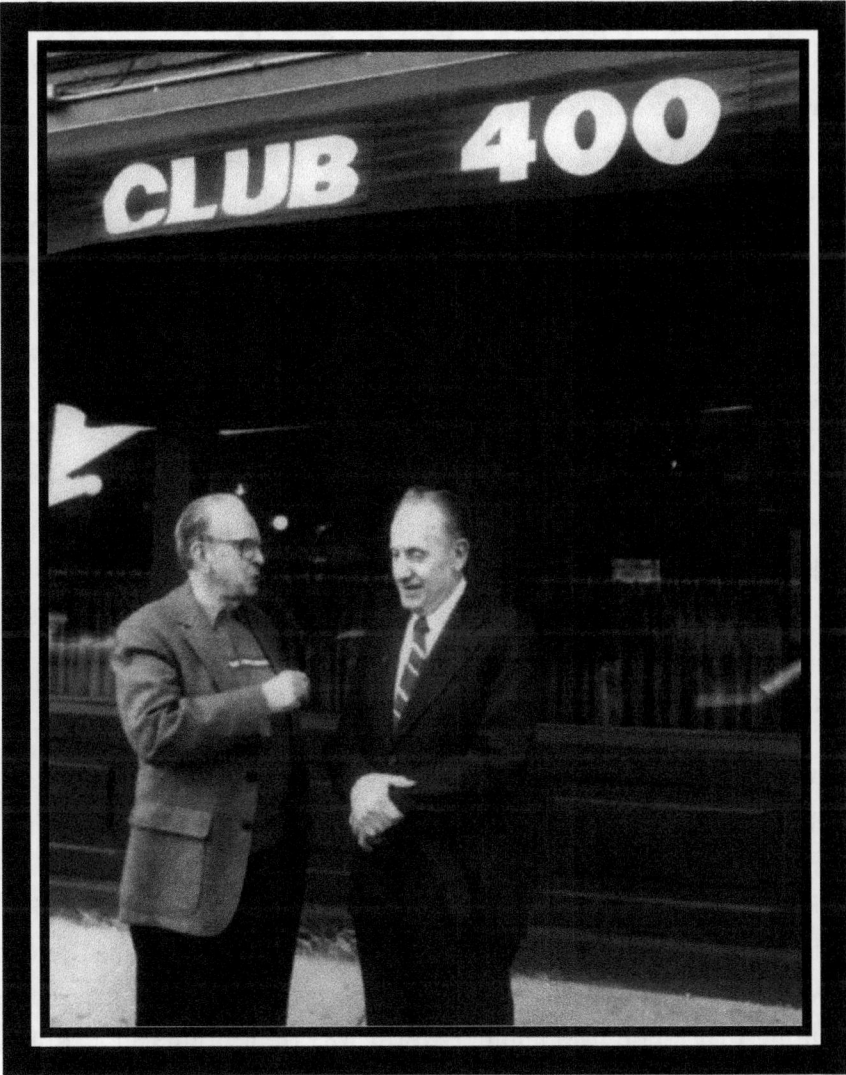

---

[6] Les Paul and Father. Photo: Club 400

With such a vibrant and storied history, it's without a doubt that perhaps some of the people that visited here over the years still visit here.

In 2021, Waukesha Ghost Walks hosted a special Friday the 13th investigation at Club 400. Joining us was a medium I've worked with on almost all investigations I've been on the last few years. Like always, he had no prior knowledge of where we were going including the city, type of building, and who would be attending. A few days prior to the investigation, the psychic informed me that wherever we were going, there is a man in the basement with a guitar. Upon entering Club 400 and seeing the Les Paul memorabilia, he informed me that was the man that he had seen just days before. As we sat in the cramped and dark basement, the psychic got the feeling that there is a portal which allows spirits to come and go to this location as they please. Which raises the question, is Les Paul still visiting Club 400 after all these years?

What's fascinating about this story is the old tunnels to Fox Head Brewery were mere feet away from where we were sitting. A portal in and of itself to another historical building. Let's not forget the train station right across the street. While it's no longer operating, it's another mode of transportation in and out of Waukesha. People were coming and going from this area for decades, it only seems fitting that a portal to another world was right in this spot. It also happens to be the most spiritually active spot in the building. Multiple people have sat in that spot and have heard their name said, seen figures out of the corner of their eye, and have made contact with various spirits.

But that's not the only spot in the building where you'd be expected to encounter a ghost.

The second story was once a boarding house and private residence to a former owner. It was also the spot where a former tenant unfortunately passed away after a shaving accident. The spirits that still linger in other areas of the bar are certainly not afraid to make you aware of their presence. The current owners have had multiple encounters with a spirit they believe could be Les Paul's mother and a former owner named Mary. Both women seem to have a watchful eye on the best interests of the bar, including renovations and special events taking place. The owners have made a special point to announce their intent with anything out of the ordinary that might be happening in hopes there is no backlash from unsuspecting spirits.

While I wish I had 100 pages to detail all the paranormal things I've encountered here, I'd certainly welcome you to take a trip to Club 400 to get your own tour and possibly experience something for yourself. Of the locations I've been able to investigate, this has to be one of my favorites because either way, you won't leave disappointed - you'll either get to see a spirit or drink one.

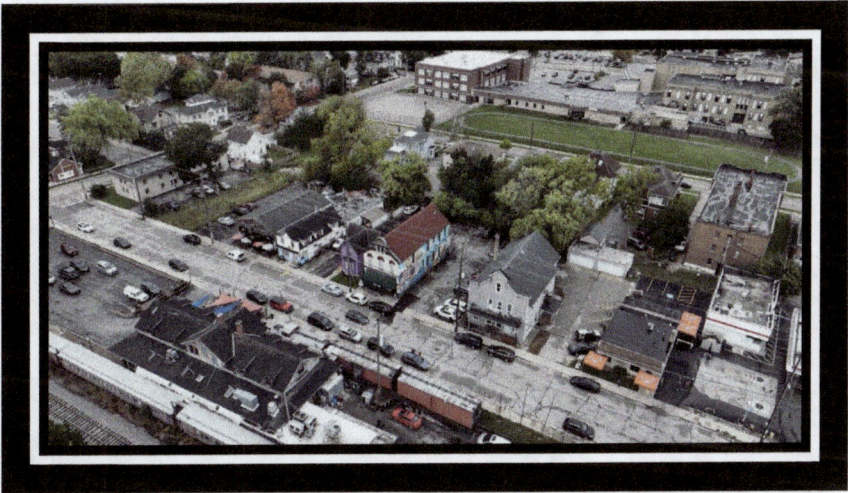

---

[7] Club 400 today. Photo: Josh Hughes

MORRIS CUTLER

[8] Morris Cutler. Photo: Waukesha County Historical Society & Museum

17

It's safe to say Waukesha quite possibly might not exist without Morris Cutler. An eccentric individual, Cutler came to this area in 1834 with his brother Alonzo. They made claim to much of the area around East, West, Wisconsin, and College Avenues. Eventually selling off most of that land made Cutler a wealthy man. While his brother wasn't cut out for the harsh Wisconsin winters, Morris stayed in Waukesha until his death in 1896.

At that time, Waukesha would have been known as Prairieville-rightly named after the famous rolling hills of the Kettle Moraine region. He was one of the only white people here during that time but with his outgoing and eccentric personality, Morris instantly bonded with the remaining Native population. The first cabin he built on his homestead, what is now Cutler Park, was where the current flagpole is. Eventually he was married and built his bride a two-story house where the current Civil War memorial stands.

As mentioned, Cutler was a colorful individual. In the book, *1880 History of Waukesha County,* he is listed as the city's very first water ferry. You would hop on down to the Fox River, pay him 10 cents, he would take off his shirt, and you would jump on his back as he ferried you across the river. Perhaps eccentric is an understatement. Above all else, Cutler was known as a truthful individual and someone you could trust. That's why when Cutler starts to tell stories about phantom Native American voices that are waking him up in the middle of the night, people listen.

As you walk through Cutler Park, you will notice three large mounds near the bandstand. These mounds would have been Cutler's former neighbors. It's here that Cutler claimed the former Potawatomi leader, *Wauk-tsha,* was buried along with his wives. He said that he could often hear the deceased leader arguing with his wives in the middle of the night. There might be some evidence to back up Cutler's claim; in that same 1880 book, they detail excavations that took place on the larger mound. They dug down far enough to find bones, believed to be human remains, laid out in a ceremonial manner. The team then packed all the dirt up proclaiming these mounds were not to be disturbed again.

While many people know Cutler Park to be famous for the white squirrels, summer bandstand concerts, and extravagant snow sculptures in the 1990's, you might also have a reason to spend some time there after dark. Perhaps you too will hear the phantom voices of a tribal leader long dead. Even if you don't, be sure to take a stroll down Maple Avenue. Go past Williams Street, over the railroad tracks, and you'll find Morris Cutler's home still standing at the next intersection. There's a newly finished plaque detailing all the important facts of Cutler's history, minus some of the more obscure and peculiar things I was able to share with you in this chapter.

---

[9] Indian Mounds in Cutler Park. Photo: Waukesha County Historical Society & Museum

TALKING TO THE DEAD

Our greatest hope in death is that it isn't the end but only the beginning of a new journey. Whether our spirit crosses over to heaven, hell, or remains stuck in limbo– there's a strong belief that we'll have some level of communication with living creatures when we leave our earthly bodies behind. While many paranormal investigations seem to be a luck of the draw whether you'll interact with a spirit, at one point in time there was a belief that you could directly tap into the other realm and talk to the dead.

Spiritualism is the belief that once we die, our spirit may be able to contact the living. In fact, Spiritualists go on to say that our spirit form is more advanced in the afterlife than when human, even having the ability to have direct influence over us as our spirit guides. While talking to spirits wasn't a new belief, the thought that you could do it theoretically anytime you wanted, was. As early as 1840, the first spirit mediums were describing people, places, and events without previously being aware of the information. This brought national attention to the movement and a spiritualist wave spread across the country.

This new radical religious movement eventually found its way to Waukesha. Right here in our backyard, Whitewater became a hub for those who wanted to learn how to be mediums. Just like that people weren't only coming to Waukesha for magical healing water, but to also attend a seance and hopefully speak to the dead.

Morris Pratt learned of spiritualism and mediumship on a trip out east. Him and his wife attended a seance and were so moved that when they returned home, they started attending demonstrations at the farm of a medium in Jefferson County. As early as 1860, Pratt was hosting his own seances and demonstrations with some of the most world renowned spiritualists. Pratt was instructed to invest in an iron mine in 1883 by his friend Mary Hayes-Chenoweth, who was a Spiritualist healer who said she was divinely inspired to mine a particular spot of land near Ashland, Wisconsin. It worked. They both became filthy rich. In gratitude for his wealth, Morris Pratt built a "temple of science" in Whitewater, Wisconsin which would later become the Morris Pratt Institute.

The Morris Pratt Institute was, simply put, a place to go to school to talk to the dead. He created a haven for spiritualists and for teaching people how to be mediums. Urban legends around Whitewater for decades have rumored that the town was founded by witches. Locals have called Whitewater, "Second Salem", because of it. The basis of those legends is most probably the Morris Pratt Institute, where Spiritualist classes continued long after the first wave of Spiritualism after the Civil War died out and before the Second Wave hit in the 1920s.

By proximity and popularity of the time, Waukesha saw its fair share of visitors looking to drink magical water and those who wanted to talk to the dead. Probably the most famous person who visited Waukesha for those two reasons was Mary Todd Lincoln. Well before the Morris Pratt Institute opened its doors, this area was a beacon of hope for those looking to speak with loved ones who have passed. After a long four years of the Civil War and losing her husband and son, Mary came to Waukesha in the summer of 1870 to drink water, heal, and hopefully receive a message from beyond the grave. It's noted in the *Waukesha Freeman* that Mary attended many seances in Waukesha and Milwaukee, but didn't mention if the results were favorable. She was also frequently seen across Waukesha but wasn't bothered by citizens.

While it's still around today, Spiritualism saw its decline as the 1800s turned to a new century. Many of the popular names of the movement came forward stating it was all a hoax from the get-go, including Maggie Fox of the infamous Fox Sisters. Her and her sister Kate helped kickstart the movement in the 1840s by claiming

---

[10] Mary Todd Lincoln. Photo: Public Domain

they could communicate with spirits through mysterious rapping sounds.

Maggie Fox made a dramatic public confession in 1888 at the New York Academy of Music. She demonstrated how she and Kate had created the rapping sounds by cracking their toe joints and dropping apples on the floor. Though Maggie later recanted this confession, both sisters ultimately died in poverty. Kate passing away during a drinking spree in 1892, and Maggie following eight months later in 1893.

When the Second Wave of Spiritualism occurred in the 1920s after the ending of World War I, another of Wisconsin's famous sons, Harry Houdini (born Erik Weisz and raised in Appleton), became a fierce opponent of fraudulent psychic mediums and spiritualists. Motivated by the loss of his mother and his initial hope to contact her, the legendary magician and escape artist quickly recognized that many mediums used tricks and deception rather than genuine supernatural abilities. Drawing on his expertise in illusion, he attended séances in disguise, exposed the methods behind slate writing, table levitation, and spirit rapping, even recreated her feats on stage to demonstrate their non-supernatural origins.

While the Morris Pratt Institute has since moved to Milwaukee, they're still open after more than a century of Spiritualism. Wisconsin also has Camp Wonewoc about seventy miles north of Madison, which has run every summer since 1993 as a special Spiritualist camp dedicated to spreading the teachings of talking to the dead.

[11] Morris Pratt Institute. Photo: Whitewater Historical Society

25

FOX RIVER AND THE WATER MAN

There are two Fox Rivers in Wisconsin. One is the famous river that goes by Green Bay, Appleton, and Oshkosh– better known as "The Fox Cities." However the Fox River that's important to this story runs right through the heart of downtown Waukesha. If you start at Moreland Bridge by the fox statue and take a stroll along the Fox River past Frame Park, you'll eventually find yourself at the end of the dam by Discount Liquor. It's this portion of the river that's seen nearly two dozen deaths since the early 1900s.

Some of those unfortunate souls that lost their lives include a man who was walking home after a New Year's Eve party after a joyous night out downtown. A few days later they found his body in the

---

¹² Fox River Postcard. Photo: Waukesha County Historical Society & Museum

river. In 2004, another man drowned while attempting to swim across the river and in 2006 five more drownings occurred in the Fox River, ranging from a two year old boy to a 47 year old man who was fishing. As of 2024, there were two additional male bodies that were pulled out of the river. Trying to find a cause for all these deaths only makes things stranger.

In the 1930s, University of Wisconsin researcher Charles Brown was trying to preserve the folklore and legends of the native tribes of Wisconsin as well as the more recent transplants from Europe. During his research he discovered a shocking similarity between folklore creatures of the two demographics. Slavic immigrants who made their way to the Midwest told a story of a mythical "Water Man" who lived in a hidden lair in the deepest part of the river. He was said to walk and talk like a normal man, with a cloak that is split in the back, but you can recognize him by the handkerchiefs in his pocket because they're always dripping wet. Fishermen who worked the river would claim that the Water Man leads people to the riverbanks before killing them and taking them to his underwater lair.

This legend seems to align with another brought down by the native tribes that originally inhabited this land. The Native people also talk of water spirits that made the area near the river a dangerous place. In Potawatomi lore, the Maneto was a green, horned serpent who would tip over your canoe, then as you tried swimming back to shore would drag you to the depths of the river.

While these are creatures of myth, it's rather interesting how two very different cultures have almost the exact same story to explain why so many people were turning up dead in the Fox River. It also seems as if both of these creatures had a taste for male flesh with almost all of the victims being men. My best advice is that if you're a man, stay clear of Frame Park late at night. You never know if your romantic late-night stroll might end up being a date with the Water Man.

[13] Fox River. Photo: Waukesha County Historical Society & Museum

29

LITTLE LORD FAUNTLEROY

The most puzzling death that took place near the Fox River was that of a little boy. To this day we still do not know the true identity of who he was and what happened to him as it remains Waukesha's most famous unsolved cold case. It was a relatively mild winter in 1921 and March 8th was like any normal Tuesday until Waukesha Police were called out to the O'Laughlin Quarry. A worker spotted a figure floating in a pond near the mine. When police arrived, they quickly discovered the body was that of a young boy and he was pronounced dead at the scene. Through their frivolous police work they determined the boy was between the age of five and seven years old and quite short. He had blonde hair and brown eyes and didn't appear to be malnourished. What really captured their attention and eventually the nation's, was his very strange attire. He was dressed in a blouse, a button up shirt, a gray sweater from, at that time, the very expensive Bradly Knitting Company. Police believed his family was either well-to-do, or he was going somewhere important where he needed to dress up for such an occasion.

As their investigation continued, police discovered something far more horrific. The back of the boy's head had been bashed in by a blunt object and there was a large amount of water in his lungs. They came to the conclusion that the boy had been murdered and then thrown into the quarry as a means of disposal.

They dubbed the boy "Little Lord Fauntleroy" due to his striking resemblance to the title character of an 1894 children's book of the same name. The name stuck and the hunt for the boy's parents and murderer was on. While there were small leads here and there, little progress was made in identifying the child. A quarry worker did come forward stating a few weeks before the boy was found, he had witnessed a young woman in a red sweater wandering aimlessly throughout the pond area. As he approached her she anxiously inquired about whether anyone had seen a little boy in the neighborhood. The worker shook his head no and the woman joined a man in a nearby car and they drove off never to be seen again.

In a desperate effort to find out the identity, the child's body was displayed in the front window of a funeral home in Downtown Waukesha. Any member of the public was invited to come by to see if they could identify the body. Unfortunately, most people were just curious and had no information to help solve the case. After less than a week, the boy's body was transported to the Weber Funeral home to be properly prepared for a burial.

A local woman was so shaken by this case, she decided to do the best she could to make things right. Minnie Conrad knows exactly where she was when the news of the dead body broke. Someone rushed into the grocery store she was shopping at and announced, "The body of a curly headed boy of age seven has been found." She could only think of her own grandsons who were of the same age and knew something had to be done. Minnie raised enough money, a whopping $170, to purchase a suit and coffin for the boy's burial in Prairie Home Cemetery. Minnie would go on to visit the gravestone every anniversary of his body being found until her own death in 1940.

Her hope was for the future stating "If I can only live long enough to hear the murderer of that boy confess and get what's coming to him, I have a feeling that someday he will come to my door and tell me why he did it." Unfortunately, that never happened. The two are buried within walking distance of each other.

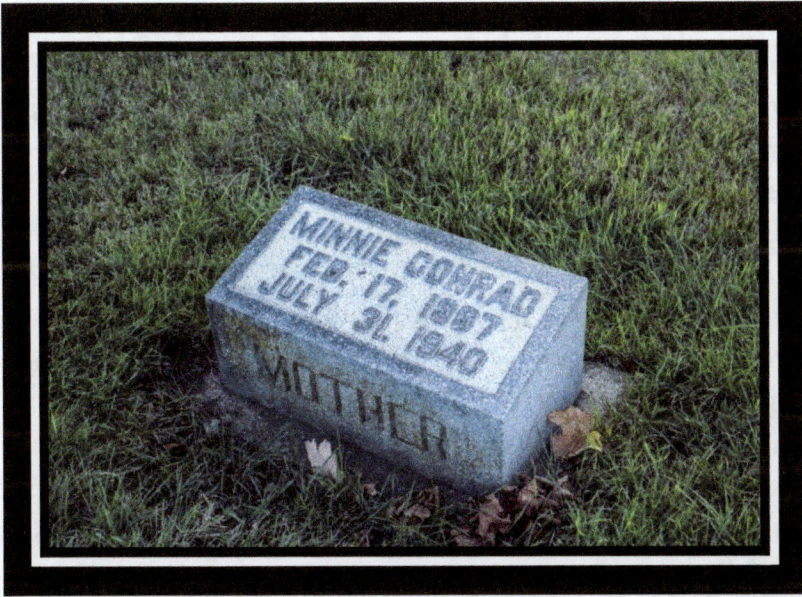

Eventually, there was hope that the case could be solved. In 1949, a medical examiner from Milwaukee believed there may have been a connection between the unknown boy and Homer Lemay, a six year old who disappeared around the same time the child died. The boy's father, Edmond, said that Homer was adopted by family from Chicago in 1921. Edmond goes on to say that the family was traveling in Argentina when Homer passed away in a car accident. Milwaukee police went on to investigate this claim by sending two detectives to South America but no proof of Homer or the accident was found.

More suspicion was brought upon Edmond when he lost a wife and another son under similarly bizarre circumstances. He defended his situation saying there was no foul play and she ran off on her own terms. Police ended up dropping dynamite in the same quarry ponds where the unknown boy was found on a tip that Edmond killed and disposed of his wife in the same manner. Their efforts were

---

[14] Minnie Conrad's Tombstone. Photo: Josh Hughes

unsuccessful. While there was not enough evidence to charge Edmond with any murder, to this day the belief is that the body found in the quarry was that of Homer Lemay. When a photograph of Edmund and the unknown boy were compared during this cold case investigation, eyewitnesses said it was an exact match of the body they viewed in the funeral parlor window.

During this same time there was a psychic named Marie St. Clair who was performing a psychic investigation on the case. Using a technique called remote viewing, she believes she was able to get into the head of the murder victim to see what happened. During this session she wrote down many things, all of it in first person as if she was there experiencing it for herself. One example from that session is as follows:

I'm in a house in a fancy parlor with lots of expensive furniture and a huge fireplace. The walls are pale. A wild navy colored carpet with a red, blue, and yellow leaf or floral pattern covers the floor. Overall, the vision is somewhat blurry. Now, I'm walking down a long hall. The same carpet covers the floor. There's an ornate stairway at the end which faces away from me. I must be back at the house. I see a slim man in a suit, neatly dressed with short hair. He has an immaculate appearance. His face is long and his eyes are dark. He looks young and then he looks old. He's at a desk before a typewriter or other machine. Maybe it's a sewing machine, I can't make it out too well.

It's a grand home. It's got a big staircase. There's a parlor and the wall is covered with trophies. Maybe he's successful, maybe he's rich, he's into politics, or maybe he's a businessman.

Then the focus shifts.

We enter a woods and I return to the woods where the man stands on the hill. He throws a body over the side. There's a brief flash of another man, burly and overweight, with long, wave reddish hair and mustache. He's about 40. I don't know who he is or what his part in this is. Perhaps he witnessed this event and never told anyone. I see a boy's dead body lying in a rocky cove or cavern- like area on a thick bed of leaves. I'm guessing that the water washes his body out from his resting place during the spring, as he was found in March.

The remote viewing session ended, and the psychic firmly believed that Edmund killed his son Homer and disposed of him in the quarry.

Like many of the stories involved with Waukesha Ghost Walks, that's where it used to end. That is until March 8, 2023 when the tradition of bringing flowers to the unknown boy's grave was revived. Yours truly was joined by American Ghost Walks friend, Jeff Finup, to bring flowers to the grave and participate in an informal investigation. While we were hoping to gain answers from any lingering spirits, the results were fruitless, yet the experience was timeless. As of 2025 we still have no answers to the identity of the unknown boy, but the mystery might be solved sooner than we think.

Many people I share this story with, on the tour and not, ask why the body isn't exhumed to conduct DNA testing. My best guess is after so much time it would be difficult, and they wouldn't want to burden ancestors with a tragedy that had nothing to do with them. But in late 2024, I decided to email the Waukesha medical examiner's office to get an answer on why they won't exhume the body and if there were future plans to do so. Below is the response I received:

Dear Mr. Hughes,

Thank you for your interest in this unknown child's case. Our office in collaboration with law enforcement, other consultants and agencies have identified several unknown decedents using DNA from disinterred remains. Regarding the child buried at Prairie Home Cemetery, we are currently working on this investigation and it is likely that disinterment will be planned at a later date.

Sincerely,

Lynda Biedrzycki, M.D.
Waukesha County Medical Examiner

Will we eventually know exactly who this unknown boy was? After all these years was it Homer Lemay that was killed by his father and disposed of in the quarry? Let's hope by the time I write a second book, we have answers to those questions.

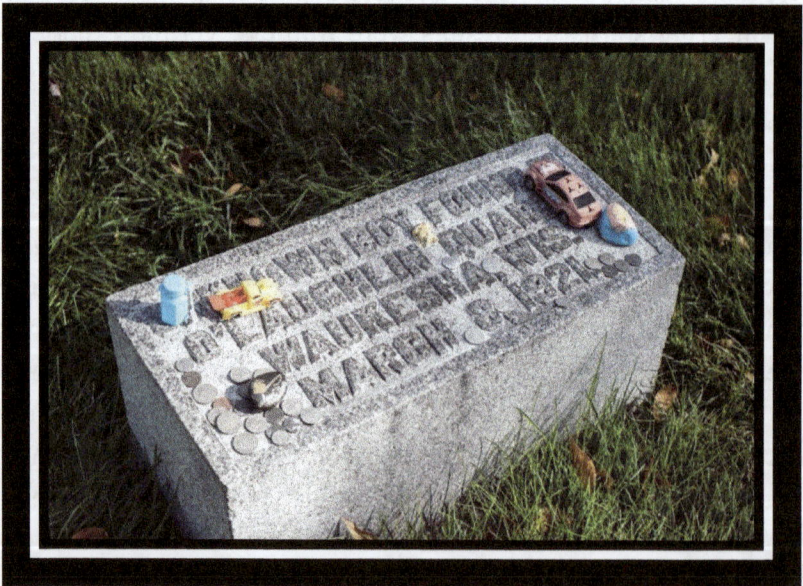

[15] The Grave of Little Lord Fauntleroy. Photo: Josh Hughes

DR. DAVID ROBERTS

[16] David Roberts. Photo: Waukesha County Historical Society & Museum

While there is no ghost involved with this next story, it just happens to be Waukesha's most infamous true crime case certainly worthy of its own Netflix adaptation. A 1971 *Waukesha Freeman* retrospect article states "Murder is news. But for murder to be a real news grabber, it should contain the following ingredients: sex (naturally), socially prominent people, and the clergy." The lack of the third ingredient should by no means diminish the quality of the lustrous tale. With equal parts romance and tragedy, it's a love triangle that ends in tragedy for some and a lesson not learned for others. It just goes to show that no matter how rich and famous you are, things can come crashing down with one bad decision.

David Roberts was at one time the most prominent veterinarian in the Midwest, if not the entire country. He can thank his upbringing for his knowledge of farming and entrepreneurial spirit. In 1850, the Roberts family settled in Racine, Wisconsin from their homeland in Wales. Farming had been in their blood for generations, so when David Roberts was born on November 10, 1865 his future had pretty much been set. When he was 18 David attended Beloit College and it was there that he would meet his first wife, Mary Newmann. The chemistry was instantaneous between the local schoolteacher and David, and they married in 1889.

Shortly after the wedding, David took a trip to Waukesha to visit his brother. After meeting many of the local farmers, he realized that there wasn't a graduate veterinarian in the city and decided to make his practice here. Saving up enough money, he was eventually able to buy a large home for himself and Mary on Wisconsin Avenue. Shortly after getting settled in, David's first book, "Practical Home Veterinarian", [a]was released in 1906. This book was essentially the bible on how to take care of your farm animals. If David wasn't well-known before this, it shot his reputation into the stratosphere.

In 1915, David would start work on his second book, *Cattle Breeds and Origin*. With such a busy work schedule, he was going to need some help. He reached out to Dr. J. E. Rogers, a professor at Carroll College, who would have been glad to help if he wasn't equally as busy. Had Dr. Rogers agreed, the rest of this story might be a moot point. Later that year, David was prompted to reach out to a local schoolteacher by the name of Grace Lusk, to help with his book. The two had met at a church social in 1914 and from his memory, she was a brilliant teacher. After approaching her, they agreed to work on the book together and the professional relationship was started.

However, shortly after spending some time together, David realized that Grace wanted much more than to write a book.

She was desperate for his attention and would go to great lengths to spend time with him. She often asked if David could take her school kids to his cattle barns which eventually led her to ask David to take her to Chicago for the weekend. Grace also would call the Roberts household all hours of the day. She was famous for hanging up immediately if David didn't answer. In May 1917, the two met in the Milwaukee Hotel for dinner. After a brief meal, Grace told David she wanted to tell him something.

"Dr. Roberts, I want you to tell me that you love me more than anybody on earth and I want you to tell Mrs. Roberts that we are in love with one another and that she must give you up."

After David refused, Grace went to the back of the room and when David turned to see her, she was holding a pistol. Grace insisted David put his hand on the bible and raise his right hand. She reiterated her previous point stating, "I want you to go home and tell Mrs. Roberts that I am in love with you and I want her to give you up. If you don't promise to do this, I will kill you and then kill myself and end it all."

Somehow David convinced Grace that after his trip out east with his wife, he would tell her. Grace put away the gun and in a few short days, the Roberts were in Boston. When they returned on June 20, 1917, Grace immediately came to their house asking if David had kept his promise. He had to break the news to her that he didn't and after a heated discussion, forced Grace to leave. However, Mary Roberts was so distraught by this situation she decided to make an appointment to see Grace the following day. An appointment that would ultimately lead to June 21, 1917 being inscribed on Mary's tombstone.

Earlier in the day, Mary had attempted to make an appointment with Grace at her school office. David got to the building ahead of time and persuaded Mary not to keep that appointment. They walked back to his office building together. After they had lunch, Mary decided she was going to keep that appointment with Grace. She walked from their home on Wisconsin Avenue through Cutler Park to East Park Avenue to meet Grace at her home. A neighbor then saw Mary go into the house by someone who opened the door from inside. Grace was the only one home.

While we don't know the exact conversation that ensued, we do know Mary called David to join them. It was at this point that Grace went up to her bedroom to grab her pistol. By the time David showed up to the home, Mary was lying in the parlor with blood flowing from her side. David quickly went to the neighbors to phone the doctor and police. By the time both arrived, Mary was dead. Grace came out of her bedroom, and they all looked up at the blood soaked woman at the top of the stairs. It appeared that after shooting Mary, Grace turned the pistol on herself. She called for David, but the doctor advised him not to and as the police officer approached the stairs. She screamed at him, "If any of you attempt to come up here and get me, I will blow my brains out."

After nearly an hour and a half of discussions with David and the police official, Grace ran into her room and closed the door. A moment later, a shot was heard. The doctor quickly ran up to the room to tend to Grace and found the shot had only taken off the end of her finger. Grace stated, "that was the most unfortunate miss I ever made."

Initially, Grace wasn't expected to recover from her wounds and spent a great deal of time telling her nurse that she hoped to die. By a stroke of luck she fully recovered and was moved to the third floor of the county jail on July 9, 1917. There had never been a woman incarcerated here, so they converted the third floor to be Grace's apartment and filled it with many of her personal effects.

Almost a full year would go by before the trial would begin on May 13, 1918. In attendance were most of Waukesha's prominent figures, Grace's dad, women's activists, and journalists from all across the nation. There was a spotlight on Waukesha and everyone wanted to get a glimpse at the world-famous veterinarian and the sex-crazed schoolteacher, as the media had labeled her. As David took the stand he painted a portrait of a delusional temptress that was constantly hounding him. Much of which Grace objected to.

When it was her turn to speak, Grace was said to have a stern yet approachable appearance for the duration of the trial. She faced a crowded courtroom and sketched her early struggles to gain an

[17] Grace Lusk. Photo: Waukesha County Historical Society & Museum

education, the vacation she spent in study, her positions as schoolteacher, and finally coming to Waukesha where she was introduced to Dr. Roberts. Early on in the trial the defense laid the foundation for the plea of insanity. Witnesses testified that her father was queer and that her mother was subject to violent bursts of passion.

Others said that for years Grace suffered from severe headaches, followed by periods of depression. The hope of proving her instance was to save her from a prison sentence. The only detailed that remained untouched was the part pertaining to the killing of Mary Roberts. Grace says she does not remember having done this. Once reminded that Grace fired one bullet into Mary's body and that she was dead, she stated that she remembers firing a second bullet to hopefully end her own life.

A motive for murder was hard to come by for the state prosecuting attorney. There was an attempt to get Grace to admit that she wanted to become Mrs. Roberts someday and eliminating Mary was the only route to take. However, Grace shot that down stating she decided to kill herself as early as May 18, 1917. She was convinced that David did not really love her and that the true love was between Mr. and Mrs. Roberts. Eventually Grace came under intense questioning and was asked if she ever intended to shoot Mary. To which she answered that she did not. It was further understood outside of the court that Grace was made desperate by anger because of unprintable names heaped upon her by Mary Roberts.

According to Grace Lusk, the monologue delivered that fateful day by Mary went something like this:

"She said the doctor did not care for me; just for sport as he had made of many other women. She told of a girl who had died as the result of an operation, and said I would die that way. She ridiculed

42

me and my friends; said I had no friends. She called me such names. She said I was nothing but an old woman, that I was running around the streets looking for a bulldog and that I was a low-life."

18

It was a sweltering day in the courtroom as the verdict was delivered. As the judge read Grace would be found guilty of second-degree murder, the narrative was instantly confirmed that Grace might be insane. She leapt across the bench and started choking and attacking the prosecuting attorney, enough to draw blood from his cheek. Grace had to be torn away by other attorneys and was carried back to her cell, shrieking. Grace was sentenced to 19 years in prison that she served at Waupun Prison.

---

[18] Grace Lusk and her lawyer. Photo: Waukesha County Historical Society & Museum

Thankfully for Grace, she only served five years of her sentence and was pardoned by the governor of Wisconsin. She would go on to marry a man only known as "Mr. Brown" and the rest of her life was relatively quiet with the exception of her dedication to prison reform. What she saw at Waupun and what she learned from other prisoners had Grace convinced she could perform a great service for the public and the unfortunate. She passed away in 1930 while David would go on to live another 23 years. After the trial David was not without punishment. He was charged with taking an unwed woman across state lines, which at the time of the trial was illegal. He served one year in a Milwaukee jail.

Once David was released he would go on to continue his business and would re-marry three times. Each marriage ended under similar circumstances with infidelity being the main issue. While he never had any kids, he did pour his heart and soul into an autobiography that was a large help in piecing together this story. It also gives you a glimpse into the mind of a man that swears "marriage is beautiful." His last wife, Elizabeth, was only 33 years old at the time of their wedding in 1948. The marriage was short-lived though, as David passed away in 1951 at the age of 85.

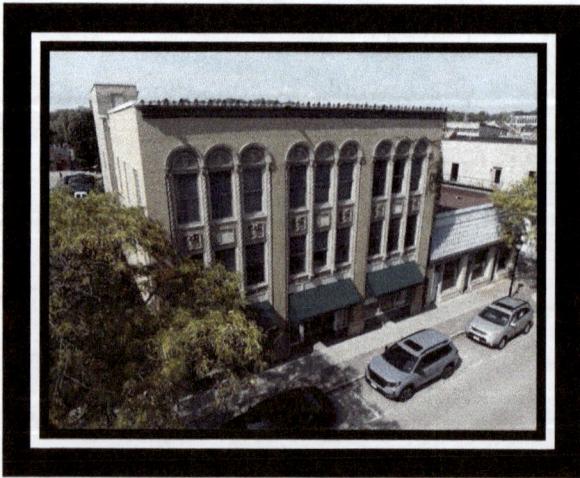

[19]

_____

[19] Dr. David Roberts' Office. Photo: Josh Hughes.

HILLE FAMILY CURSE

Curse /kərs/*
Noun
1. intended to invoke a supernatural power to inflict harm or punishment on someone or something.

About 10 miles outside of Waukesha on River Road sits a timeless farmhouse on 150 acres of farmland. Those that have lived in the nearly 200-year-old farmhouse don't doubt for a second that the house and land are cursed. Of the families that have lived there over the years, twelve of them were handed strange and untimely deaths. There have been accidents, drownings, murders, others were gored by animals, blown up, crushed, poisoned… and some killed themselves. While the stories of these people have generated some eye grabbing newspaper headlines, we have very little visual reference of their existence.

This is a story of the American Dream that ended in tragedy. When families came to this farm to seek a peaceful and fruitful existence only to be met with disaster. Those who lived there were warned by the living… and the dead, that this place was evil. While the reason for the curse is up for speculation, the origins of it might lie with the people that called Waukesha home well before it was given the name.

Native Americans, specifically the Potawatomi tribe, had called this area home since the 1600s. The belief is that at one point in time the land where this story takes place was once inhabited by the native population that was displaced after wars with the Iroquois Confederacy. While I can't say for certain from my research, I've had multiple sources tell me that a curse was given to the land by a former Native American tribe. While I wouldn't agree that the land was actually cursed, we can say there was a high probability that native remains were buried on this property at one point in time. Of which we know there are other consequences for disturbing human remains. In that regard, I would say there very well could be restless spirits responsible for unfortunate incidents that took place.

Now the curse wasn't always present, but it affected one family more than the rest. Four family members were claimed, all under very bizarre circumstances. It all starts with a man seeking his slice of American pie.

John Hille was born in Hanover, Germany in 1811. He eventually immigrated to New York where he met his wife Mary and married in 1842. While her obituary states they had two children before moving to Wisconsin, there are many inconsistencies from 180 years ago. In the obituary of John Hille it states the couple came to Waukesha as early as 1843. However we do know their first child, John Hille Jr. was born in 1844 and by the time their second child Elizabeth was born, they had moved to the town of Waukesha.

As Wisconsin was officially named a state in 1848, the Hille family were planting their roots along the Fox River on what would eventually be named River Road. They built this home in addition to multiple barns and outbuildings. Joining their family between 1850 and 1862 would be six more children– Edwin, Anna, Hulda, Lillie, William, and Oscar.

John Hille came to America and eventually Waukesha to have his version of the American dream. That includes owning a farm, having lots of children, and being an upstanding member of the community. For a number of years, John and his family had exactly the life they dreamed of. As stated in his obituary, "He always had those sterling qualities of citizenship which are a pride to all...a

Teutonic pioneer of Waukesha." Obviously of German descent, John was proud and often celebrated his German heritage as a member of the Germania Singing Society.

The first reported death on the property was that of the eldest son, John Hille Jr. in 1873. Beyond that, we know very little of his life and circumstances surrounding his death. We do know he was a Civil War veteran and is buried with the family in Prairie Home Cemetery. In hindsight, the curse was born or at least claimed the first victim that we're aware of in 1874. All we know from a Waukesha Plaindealer newspaper clipping is that Thomas Reese was fishing in the Fox River on Mr. Hille's property and drowned.

It wasn't until the passing of Mary Hille that the people of Waukesha started to get suspicious of something odd going on at the Hille farm. Leading up to her death, Mary was ill for most of 1882. Mr. Hille phoned Dr. Hugo Philler who was a practitioner and a popular professor of Latin and German at Carroll College. A short time after arriving on the farm, Mary was dead before the doctor could even realize the mistake he made. He had accidentally given Mary morphine instead of quinine to treat her illness. Although she was extremely ill and would have only lived a few months longer, this mistake ended up killing the matriarch of the family. Unfortunate and untimely, it was with this death that rumors of a curse on the Hille farm began to make their way through Waukesha.

At this point, John was advanced in age and ended up moving to a home on East Park Avenue with his two daughters, Anna and Lillie. Passing away in 1903 at the ripe age of 92, he was listed in a newspaper clipping as a pioneer of Waukesha joined by a few others who had passed in what they called at the time "an unusual number of deaths." What I find even stranger is that of all the gentlemen listed in the article, John Hille is the only one that doesn't have his photograph printed.

By the time the curse would claim its next victim, it had been dormant for 33 years. Once it woke up, it claimed nine more lives in a timespan of three years.

The first being Oscar Hille. It was a Sunday morning on June 6, 1915. Oscar was in the pasture when a vicious bull attacked him. It tore open his chest, spilling out his guts, and he bled to death right there in the field. Now I used to work as a journalist and I know from time to time you do need to sensationalize things. This is exactly what the *Waukesha Freeman* did. In fact, his brother and sister were so adamant to get the story straight, they actually had the *Freeman* reprint Oscar's obituary stating, "He went out to the barn, untied one of their bulls, and took him out for exercise and eating. While playing, the bull got excited and crushed Oscar's arm against the barn." At that time you can assume Oscar was quite scared, perhaps he even screamed. The bull became unmanageable but eventually Oscar was able to get him back into the barn and tied up. He made it into the house and called his siblings and the doctor. However, poor Oscar died a few days later from what they believed at the time was internal bleeding.

Regardless of what exactly happened, you know that people talk and gossip. Once word spread across Waukesha that the curse was alive and claiming lives again, all the hired hands on the farm quit, leaving William and Hulda Hille to find help elsewhere. That brings us to 1918 which ends up being the most deadly and confusing year on this property.

As we all know our world history, this was the last year of The Great War. It had been a worrisome four years for William and Hulda Hille on their family farm. With their mother from France and father being from Germany, there was suspicion of who their loyalty was with. At the time, the public had no reason to question which side the Hilles were on, as they gave generously to the U.S. war effort purchasing a hefty amount of Liberty Bonds. All that aside, they rarely trusted anyone and finding good help was hard. Only two people were hired to work on the farm. One was a neighbor boy named Fentz who lived down the road. He would perform odd jobs around the property. They also hired a farm hand from Milwaukee named Krause who had to convince the Hille siblings to hire him. A decision they would ultimately come to regret and pay for with blood.

July 11, 1918 ended up being the most tragic and bizarre day yet on the farm. Krause showed up for his morning duties and revealed the sinister intentions behind his reason for wanting to work for the family. He knocked on the front door and as William answered, Krause cleared his throat and stated, "I am a U.S. Secret Service agent and I'm here on suspicion that you and your sister are German sympathizers."

Krause threatened to expose William and Hulda to which they responded by giving Krause thirty dollars to keep his mouth shut.

Obviously, he was fired and he went skipping down the dirt road into Waukesha with his money. As he was doing so, he ran into the other farm hand, Fentz. Explaining the situation, Fentz licked his lips and said "they are worth a hell of a lot more than that. Let's go back and try to get some more money." Devious plans cooked up by a teenage boy and a man with a criminal past.

They walked back to the Hille farm and knocked on the front door for a second time, but there was little discussion to be had. An argument quickly broke out between the three. Panicked, Hulda called their neighbor Pearl Dingledine and asked for her to hurry over. Just as she stepped foot in the house, a shot was heard from the back of the home. William walked from the kitchen to greet Pearl. He offered to shake hands but she refused and attempted to grab the shotgun. Hulda stepped in and stated "Let him go, it's for the best. They are after us anyways. And you cannot prevent this. We will be dead before anyone can get here."

William walked outside and made his way toward the barn. In the distance, Krause could be seen running down the dirt road. Pearl was attempting to stop what she figured was the inevitable slaughter of the animals when William said, "they are after me." The two stared at each other for a moment before he marched to the barn. As Pearl turned to go back home, Hulda grabbed her by the arm and shoved a wooden box in her hands. The contents of that box will be important in the aftermath of this event.

However, before Pearl could get there, five more shotgun blasts echoed to her property. She made haste by calling the police, but it would be more than two hours before they could arrive at the Hille farm. When the police finally arrived, the property was silent. They started with the house where they found the neighbor boy, Fentz, slumped over in a rocking chair in the kitchen. His face was barely recognizable.

They made their way outside and into the barn where they found five horses and the family dog all with a bullet hole in the back of their heads behind the ear. The police then made their way upstairs, where they found Hulda dead in her bed with a razor blade in one hand and a vile of poison on the chair nearby. In the other bedroom was William with a bullet wound to his chest and the shotgun on the floor at his feet.

In a matter of sixty minutes, three people were dead– two by suicide, and six animals were slaughtered as well.

The farm hand, Krause, was found two days later in St. Paul. In that time he had fled Waukesha, enlisted in the military, and was en route to a North Carolina military base when he was apprehended and brought back to Milwaukee. He was of little help to make sense of this tragedy. He was eventually charged with blackmail and spent time in jail.

The remaining Hille family members Anna, Lillie, and Elizabeth, were of little help in the situation. They were completely taken aback by the situation stating their brother and sister were of sound mine, had no influence from Germany, and William was actually quite good friends with the neighbor boy Fentz. However, the coroner's report, death records, and testimony from the neighbor woman Pearl painted a much clearer picture of the situation. William died by suicide from a 12-gauge shotgun. Hulda, suicide by poison (said to be "mentally deranged"). Ernest Fentz, gunshot wound, probably in the hand of William Hille.

The contents of that wooden box are the key to unlocking this mystery.

In addition to a few personal items, the deed to the land, and bank statements, there was a very bizarre letter that Hulda had written one week earlier after waking up in the middle of the night and hearing a thumping noise on the wall. She believed this was a sign that misfortune was heading their way. It reads:

"Say girls, the other night there was a slapping noise on the wall. I knew what that meant, so goodbye. All be good with Eliza. There are only these three left. We will try our best to get our rights. Don't take it hard because Bill (William) would have to be in prison for life; he was telling Bill about the Japs coming over and how they will come. And then Bill – we would go in the house and shoot them. Give the machine to H. and A. That is W's wish."

On the opposite side was written:

"Ally and John, Arthur and Willie, Jamy and Will Werning for pall bearers."

There's a lot to unpack with this suicide note. Digging into historical context, there is no real threat with the Japanese since this was well before World War II. Every person listed on the first side is part of the Hille family. William, referred to as Bill and W, and Elizabeth Hahn nee Hille who was the only Hille sibling to have children. H and A would have been Hulda's niece and nephew. The back side listed farmers that lived around Waukesha County.

After this incident, the curse was apparent, and the property became undesirable. Between 1918 and 1950 the curse continued to strike those who were brave enough to traverse the property. There was a young family that lived there for a short time. They lost two infants to crib death. There was also another man who was renting the farm fields - he ended up losing his life in an unfortunate dynamite accident attempting to blow up a boulder.

The property then sat empty until a family from Chicago purchased the property and spent the next four years renovating it. Ralph and Dorothy Ransome renamed the property Ravensholme and eventually invited their daughter and her new husband to join them on the farm in 1953. Anita and Andrew Kennedy had been made aware of the supposed curse on the farm but chose not to believe it. Whether that was to not give power to it in hopes of avoiding the curse, we often find these things have more power over us than we think.

The first tragedy that struck the Kennedy family was in 1963. While it didn't take place on the property, it was certainly untimely, nonetheless. Seven-year-old Phillip Kennedy was swimming in Lake Mendota at a retreat and drowned. Nine years later the last reported death took place on the property. In 1972, four-year-old Ransome Kennedy was playing in the barn and as he attempted to step over an auger, he slipped and fell into the machine. He was crushed to death.

Up to this point, there's been no ghost story, if you haven't noticed. But it's with this last death that we finally get a glimpse of the supposed ghost of John Hille on the farm. During 1972, Dorothy Ransome reported seeing a black shadowy figure roaming the farm. Sometimes it would be so quick that she couldn't make out any features, other times she could clear as day tell it was an old man in a black coat with a black hat. She believed this was the ghost of John

---

[20] Ravensholme as it looks today. Photo: Josh Hughes

Hille. While most of the sightings seemed to be harmless, Dorothy believes the appearance one week before Ransome's death was a warning that something bad was about to take place on the farm. She saw the ghost many times after that last death, but this was the only time she felt a foreboding energy.

---

[21] Anita and Dorothy Ransome. Photo: Waukesha County Historical Society & Museum

As of 2024, Ravensholme is still an active farm although the farmhouse has since been divided into a duplex. While inside no longer has that old world charm, the farmhouse on River Road looks exactly like it did when John Hille built it. Over the years I've been able to speak with several previous tenants who were shocked to hear of the tragic stories that took place on the farm. While nothing alarming enough occurred while they lived there, in hindsight a few creepy things came to mind. Most notable shadow figures in the farm fields and phantom smells including coffee when no one was brewing any.

My journey to step foot on this property eventually came true in 2024. In a most selfless act, Anita donated the farm land and house to Tall Pines Conservancy, a non-profit land trust focused on preserving the Lake Country region and beyond. This ensures the historical property will remain intact forever. I saw this as an opportunity to not only learn more about their historical preservation but to potentially visit the property and meet Anita. All of that came true within a matter of months as the Conservancy was very receptive to the idea as was Anita.

Through my previous discussions with tenants of the property, they advised me to make no mention of the ghost stories as Anita was a firm believer that all those tales were made up. Regardless, I still saw this as an opportunity to interact with a first-hand witness, learn about the history of the property, and learn more about the future of the land.

The former farmhand house is where Anita currently resides, about a mile from the farm she recently donated. As I entered the front door, she greeted me with a slight smile and a firm handshake. I started out by showing her a book that was left in my house from the previous owners. "A Day in the Life" was a glimpse into everyday life of Waukesha citizens and published by Waukesha State Bank in 1988. In this book is a photo of Anita's mother standing outside the farmhouse and a photo of a former farmhand. As Anita's fingers scanned the words, she confirmed the information on the page, even recalling the personality of the farmhand.

The description on the page ends with the tragic death of Anita's younger son and the story of how her mother believes she saw a ghost on the property. It was at this moment that Anita turned to me and asked, "Do you believe in ghosts?" I answered with a simple yes and she smiled once again. "I don't believe in ghosts, and I never saw a ghost there." Since the focus of this meeting was not to decide whether ghosts exist, I left it at that.

The interview lasted about an hour. We talked about her family history, her time on the farm with her parents, the tragic loss of two sons, her donation of the property, and her hopes for the future of the land. My intent of meeting Anita was not to discuss the ghost stories associated with the Hille farm. This was purely to learn about her first-hand experience on this historical farm.

The paranormal field has so many elements to it and the one I find the most interesting is the history. You can quite literally take a step back in time and visit another era while learning more about these stories. Immersing yourself in the research is quite possibly the closest thing to time travel that we might ever get to experience. It's rare that we get to be in the presence of someone who lived through these events. Having the opportunity to interview Anita and learn a glimpse of what she went through was a moment that I will forever get to cherish. Even though we don't share the same beliefs about the afterlife we most certainly have the same appreciation of history and preservation.

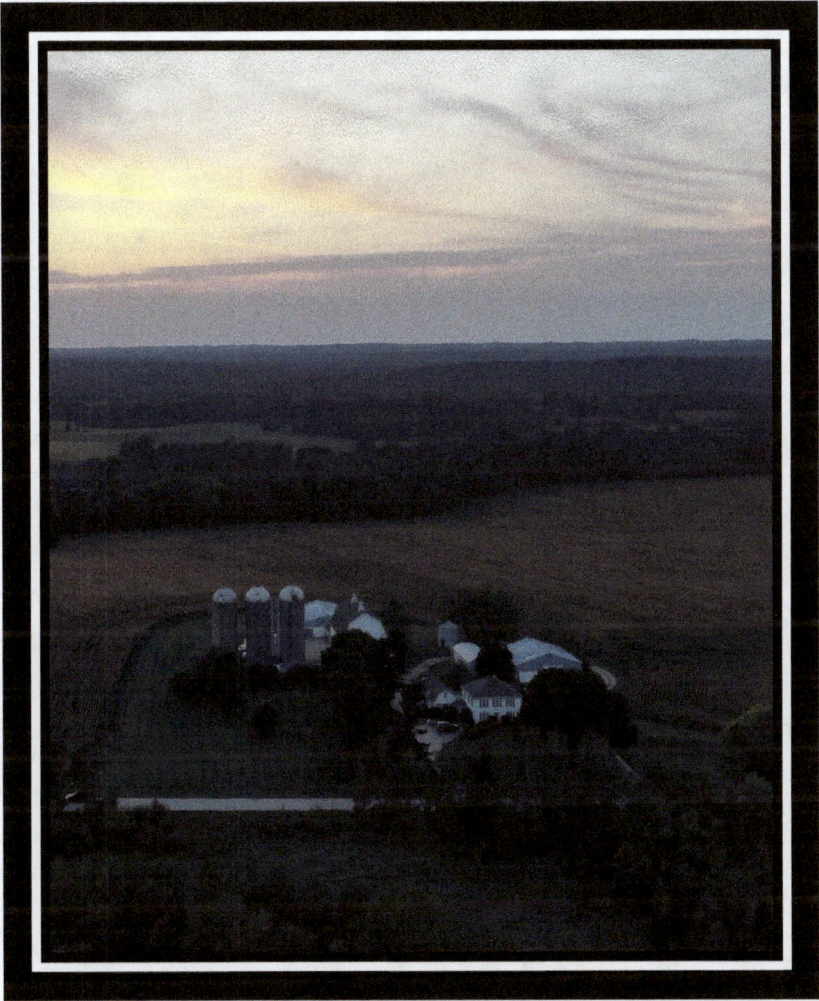

---
[22] An aerial view of Ravensholme. Photo: Josh Hughes

CARROLL UNIVERSITY

[23] MacAllister Hall at Carroll University. Photo: Josh Hughes

You would not have Carroll without Waukesha and without Waukesha, you might not have Carroll. Nestled in the middle of a historic neighborhood sits Wisconsin's oldest institute of higher learning. Carroll College, as it was known up until 2008, was established in 1846 just two years before Wisconsin was a state. The first year had only five students and two faculty members. The most prominent building on campus is Main Hall, with the current iteration of it has been there since 1887. The original Main Hall burnt down in 1885. It's built entirely of limestone much like many of the older buildings on campus. If you take a walk on the grounds you won't only notice the old buildings and houses, but also a number of mounds that decorate the landscape. These are Native American effigy mounds that they believe date back to 750 A.D. This entire area was mapped by A. Lapham in the 1850s and these aren't the only mounds you can find on College Hill.

Being the oldest university in the state, with buildings made of limestone and effigy mounds surrounding your campus, you can expect several ghost stories to exist. One of the main reasons I think so much energy remains on this campus is for those two reasons. Some believe limestone possesses the ability to absorb and "replay" past events and emotions almost like a recording - this is called Stone Tape Theory. Since most of the campus buildings are made of limestone, especially the ones I had the most encounters in, you can go out on a limb and say these areas are more prone to hauntings. In fact, most of the buildings surrounding campus including homes and businesses have—at the very least—limestone foundations. This makes the area ripe for a supernatural encounter.

Much like any old college, there's always a good ghost story that gets passed around the Halloween season. Many of those are exaggerated stories that seem to grow deeper in lore as each person tells it to the next. However, I can tell you from firsthand experience, there is certainly some truth to the spirits that linger in the halls and grounds of Carroll University.

There is a large house that sits on the corner of East Avenue and East College Avenue. It's here at MacAllister Hall that the most well-known ghost story of Carroll University resides. The home was built by Geoge Wilbur in 1895. He owned a local lumber dynasty known as The Wilbur Lumber company. His second wife, Harriet, passed away in the home in 1919 and the funeral was at the residence. George followed in passing a few years later in 1922. The home was then purchased by Lydia Morgan and donated to Carroll to become a Civil War museum and library. It was renamed Morgan Manor. For a number of years that is what remained, until the 1950s when it was renovated to house students as a dormitory. Quickly after moving in, the students gave it the proper nickname "The Morgue" because they said they were experiencing ghosts.

Some of the stories include objects moving, phantom smells, lights turning on and off, and some said they saw Mr. and Mrs. Weber floating down the staircase in nightly attire before disappearing out the front door. One of the more bizarre stories (that we know is made up) is students saying they saw Lydia Morgan floating around the house with a noose around her neck. We know that to be fake because she did not commit suicide or live in the house.

What I think to be the most compelling of these stories occurred in 1972 when Joe Kremkowski had a terrifying experience. Joe was frequently being awoken in the middle of the night by something grabbing his foot. Eventually when he woke up fast enough to look towards the end of his bed, he saw a man smiling before disappearing into the night. When he shared this story with his peers, they encouraged him to do some research on who this playful foot grabber might be. Upon browsing through a Wilbur Lumber Company brochure, the student pointed to Ray Wilbur as the foot grabber. Ray was the son of George and would go on to run the company for a number of years after his father's death.

Eventually students moved out of Morgan Manor. It was renamed MacAllister hall and renovated into classrooms and office space. However, the stories of ghosts haunting the mansion didn't cease to exist. Students would eventually conduct an official paranormal investigation, but did not report anything abnormal occurring besides having their electronic devices lose battery quickly.

During my second year as the tour guide for Waukesha Ghost Walks, a former staff member stopped me after this story and informed me there were "a lot more frightening things occurring at Carroll." They then invited me on a personal late night tour of the entire campus so that they could share everything they had experienced in their time there. The following stories happened during that private tour where we had full permission to enter the buildings of Carroll University.

We started our tour in Main Hall, the icon of Carroll. There has always been this tale amongst students that if you find yourself in the building late at night, you can see a woman in a Victorian era dress standing in the tower. I have no evidence to back this up and it seems it might purely be a myth. However, I can personally attest to weird activity, as we all participated in a ghost box session on the third floor next to an old Carroll College bench. We received multiple responses on command of something still referring to this place as Carroll College. A ghost box scans through radio channels at a high rate to create a white noise, allowing intelligent spirits to communicate with us. Sometimes you might get bits and pieces of songs or advertisements that answer your questions but I've also heard phantom voices through this device.

As we moved throughout the campus, the staff member told me one of the most bizarre things they and many of their co-workers witnessed all across campus was a kid wearing a red hooded sweatshirt. As soon as they approach this person or try to communicate, the kid would vanish. While that's certainly not enough to go off of, it made sense a year later when I returned to Carroll with another staff member I met on a tour. This time we returned with a psychic medium to hopefully get some more answers. I would like to preface this story with how my medium and I operate. Whenever I ask him if he's available, we meet at a neutral site. Then I drive us to the location without giving him any hints of the location, whether it be a house, bar, church, etc. As we approached the university, the psychic explained he was receiving visions of Native Americans, fitting for Carroll.

The tour was quicker than the first I had taken and became forever engrained in my memory when we reached the most interesting portion of Main Hall - the basement. The medium walked past desks in the dimly lit classroom, explaining that he saw classes being held here over the years. He referred to it as a time stamp, things that were not interacting with each other and were oblivious to us being there. He suddenly stopped.. He pointed to the middle of the room and said, "There was one kid who knows who we are and why we're here." I asked what the kid was wearing and he responded, "a red hooded sweatshirt pulled up over his head."

My heart just about fell into my butt.

As I was focusing my camera, I asked why the kid was here. From what the psychic gathered, this student had done something to end his life and now was stuck here in eternal regret. As we made our way through campus to different spots, he would note that the kid was here, and there, and also went to other buildings from time to time. Carroll was now his forever home and he wishes he could take back the decision he made. While I haven't been able to corroborate any of these stories with factual events, it certainly does give potential context to the same kid the other employees had been seeing over the years.

What makes Carroll University unique is that the academic buildings almost seamlessly blend with the surrounding homes. Many of these former residences that have been acquired by the university are now office buildings for faculty and staff.

Just two blocks down from MacAllister Hall is McCall and East Avenue. On that corner sits another large home on top of a small hill. Behind it are more historic homes and to the side, a parking lot and dormitory.

Although I was touring this home with no paranormal intent, walking from the attic to the second floor I heard a door on the first floor open and slowly close. I quickly pulled out my ghost radar and asked if anyone was present. The two words that came through this device led me to research that might explain spirits that cling to this house. The first word was "daughter" and a minute or so later "fall" came through. To me, these words didn't seem random and I had enough to go off of. I found the home was built in 1892 and the original owner did have a daughter that died at a young age. Even more fascinating is that the owner, a local doctor, suffered a terrible death in that very house where I heard the door open.

It was October 1898 when Dr. John Wigginton was walking up the front steps and he realized the door was locked. His son yelled from the second story that he would come let him in, but Wigginton refused and walked around to the side door. After entering the home, the son heard a noise; upon walking downstairs, he found his father dead on the bathroom floor. He had slipped and died on impact. The two random words certainly didn't seem so random anymore.

THE PUTNEY HOUSE

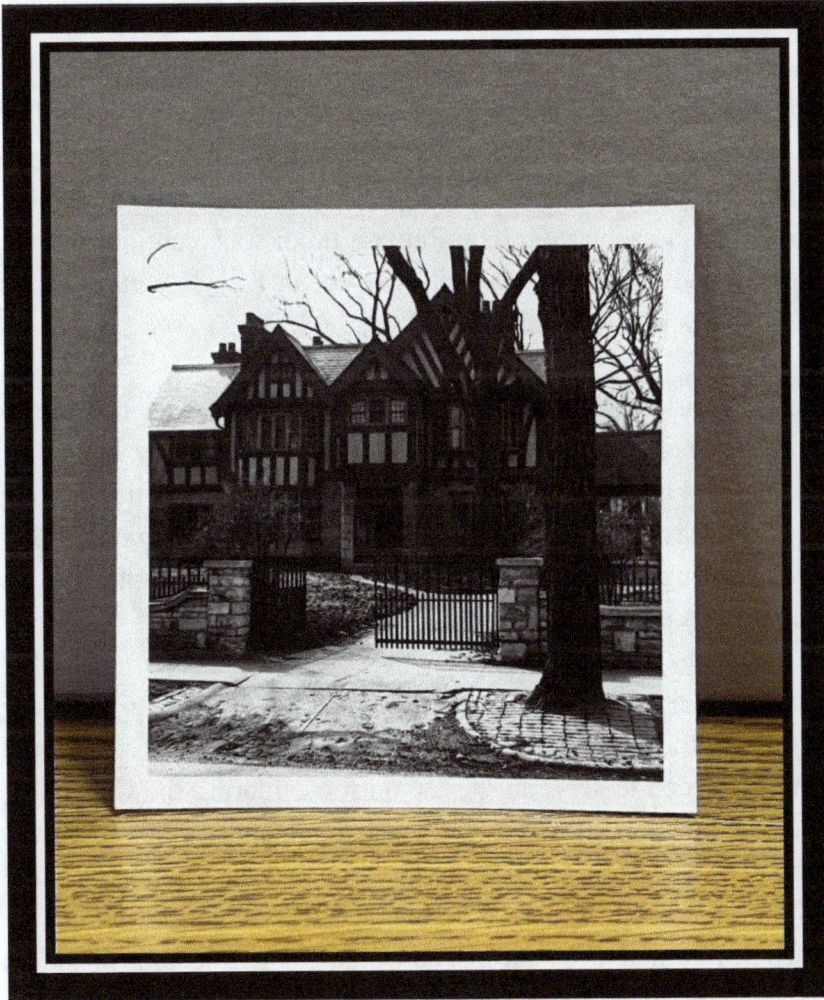

If you're driving down Wisconsin Avenue and blink at just the right time, you might miss an old colonial house sandwiched between the

---

[24] Putney House. Photo: Waukesha County Historical Society & Museum

former Eric's Porter Haus and a four-story commercial building. The house in question is so camouflaged by vines that it blends right in with its environment. While some haunted houses want to hide their dark past, this one should celebrate and promote the apparent paranormal visitations by one of Waukesha's most cherished citizens.

Frank Putney built the home at 223 Wisconsin Avenue in 1901. A man who made his mark as one of the greatest city leaders in late nineteenth century Waukesha. In Frank's obituary, it is mentioned that his family can trace their history back to the original settlement in Salem, Massachusetts. John Putney Junior was mentioned in the records of the Salem Witch Trials. It wasn't for witchcraft, but he did receive a painful punishment.

The Puritans and Quakers did not mess around when it came to punishing bad behavior and in the case of John Putney Junior, he was branded like cattle. A hot iron in the form of a letter designating the crime was held on his forehead until he uttered the words "God save the King." John Putney Junior got a "B" for burglary. A bit extreme of a punishment if you ask me!

Frank was a few generations removed and was an upstanding member of the community. Frank studied law at Carroll College and then proceeded to serve in the Union forces during the Civil War, where he fought in the Siege of Vicksburg and the Battle of Atlanta. Putney even served during Sherman's famous March to the Sea, the brutal campaign that helped demoralize the South and win the war. When he returned to Waukesha, he would go on to become president of the village, the postmaster, and even the county judge.

When Frank died in 1914, the *Waukesha Freeman* called this house "possibly the finest example of architecture in the city." It would eventually pass through Frank's family and in 1990 served as the home for the Waukesha Chamber of Commerce. A huge portrait of Frank Putney used to hang in the house's dining room, which served as the staff conference room.

While Frank had been deceased for decades, he may have been watching them in more ways than that. While the Waukesha Chamber of Commerce had its office here, people would hear strange voices coming from rooms where there was no one there. Footsteps would go up and down the old staircases that didn't have any human feet attached. Employees would lose belongings for weeks at a time, only to find them in the same place they left. They said they felt a mischievous presence in the home, but nothing concerning.

As of 2025, the building is home to a dental clinic and an addiction recovery clinic. I was fortunate enough to have the dentist that owns this practice on my tour during one of my first summers. It wasn't until the tour was done that he told me this and informed me that while he had heard the story before, he and his staff hadn't experienced anything for themselves.

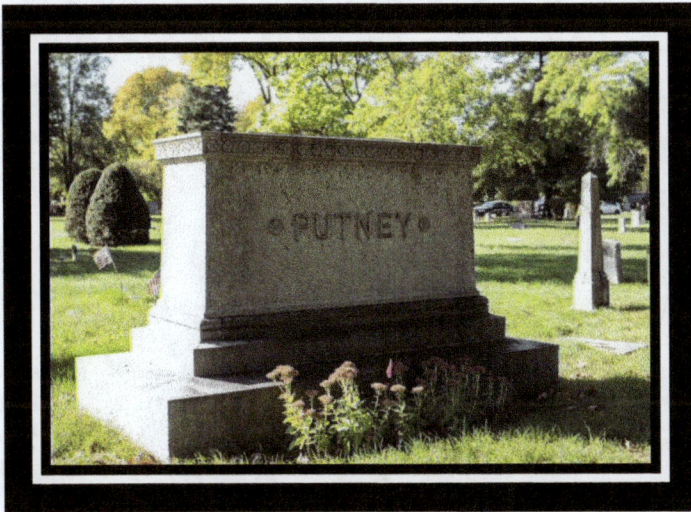

[25] Putney Tombstone. Photo: Josh Hughes

THE WITCH HOUSE

Try to picture that one house in your childhood neighborhood that seemed to make everyone uncomfortable. Even though it's Halloween, you think twice about going to the front door to say, "trick or treat." Sure, it seems silly, but all stories are rooted in some amount of truth, right? Especially the types of stories that spread amongst your group of friends like wildfire. Something about a glowing blue skull you can see in the backyard on Friday the 13th and how it might have to do with the witch that used to live there.

While I can't say for certain if you'll experience a witch or a glowing blue skull, I can say from experience there is still something haunting the house on Rosemary Street.

The home had a non-traditional beginning. Per the current owners, it might have been built as a model home for a failed housing subdivision venture. The property changed hands a few times, with it being lived in very little, until Charles Merten purchased it in 1907 and his family lived there for the next 80 years. He lived there with his wife Emily and son Byron. Charles passed away in 1953, leaving Byron to care for his aging mother.

Unfortunately, her life was of poor quality until her death in 1963. Emily started exhibiting signs of dementia and wasn't too friendly with the neighbors. She was frequently seen in the front yard in her nightgown yelling at neighborhood kids to "get the hell out of her yard" when they were clear as day on their own property. Due to her old age and deteriorating condition, rumors started that there was a witch living on Rosemary Street.

With her health getting worse, Byron was forced to keep his mother in her bedroom for the rest of her life. But that didn't stop her from letting people know they needed to stay away from her house. Kids would stand on the sidewalk taunting her as she stood behind her bedroom window, screaming at the glass and poking it with her bony

---

[26] Charles, Emily, and Byron Merton. Photo: Maria and Reginald Sprecher

finger. Eventually Emily did pass in 1963, but the stories of the witch didn't stop. Many neighborhood kids refused to go past this house on Halloween, stating that it was haunted. Parents even started to believe the rumors, as many of them said they too saw the figure of a woman in the upstairs bedroom window.

While Byron's body was taken from the house when he died in 1987, all of his belongings stayed because there was no one to claim them. The house sat vacant for two years, partly because there was a reputation that the house was indeed haunted. It took a family from out of town to finally purchase the home in 1989. But as the U-Haul pulled up, they didn't take their first steps over the threshold with boxes in hand. The new family sent a priest ahead of time to bless the home since they had heard the rumors of it being haunted and certainly did not want to take any chances. The current owners purchased the home in 2000 and have restored it to its natural beauty.

Like many of my tales, that's where the story used to end. That is, until 2022…

Out of the blue, I got an email from Maria and Reginald Sprecher who currently live in the house on Rosemary Street. They had heard of the story I tell on the Waukesha Ghost Walks tour and invited me over to tour the property for myself. Let me tell you, stepping into this home is like a trip back in time. They have lovingly restored the house inside and out, paying special attention to detail and authenticity. They also have an eclectic taste for decorations with more than a dozen crystal skulls and Ouija boards scattered about the home.

The tour itself was equal parts historical journey and swapping of ghost stories. While I knew an incredible amount of historical information about the house, their personal experiences over the last 22 years makes an incredible addition to the story. One of my favorite experiences they shared with me involves the hot water

---

[27] Charles Merten. Photo: Maria and Reginald Sprecher

heater pilot light frequently going out when they first moved there. Eventually after Reginald had to re-light it multiple times, they boldly yet respectively told Byron to knock it off, this was their house now. After that day, it stayed on indefinitely.

As we walked upstairs to Emily's bedroom, they had a handful of photos sprawled out across their bed. Byron was a photographer and well known across Waukesha. Much of his photography stayed with the house and remained in the attic, while some of it was donated to the Waukesha County Historical Society. It was exhilarating to see the photo of the Witch for myself and I'll let you be the judge whether you think she practices witchcraft or not. Eventually as the tour wrapped up, we stopped into the back bedroom and that's where things got very interesting.

Anyone who's been on a paranormal investigation, visited, or lived in a haunted house knows that energy plays a large part in any interaction. Whether that be temperature changes, batteries draining power, interaction with our investigation tools, or simply the energy of a room can drastically feel different. When I stepped in that back bedroom it was as if I were walking through a thick fog. I immediately felt a shift in energy; it did not feel pleasant. I remarked to the Sprechers how different it felt and Maria let out a nervous chuckle stating, "Anyone that has spent the night here has been woken up in the middle of the night by something telling them to get out of their house." The bedroom is not very big and has an odd shaped closet in the back left corner. As I walked in there, it felt even more weird than the bedroom itself. I asked what was with the closet and all they could say was that the previous owners had that space "exorcised."

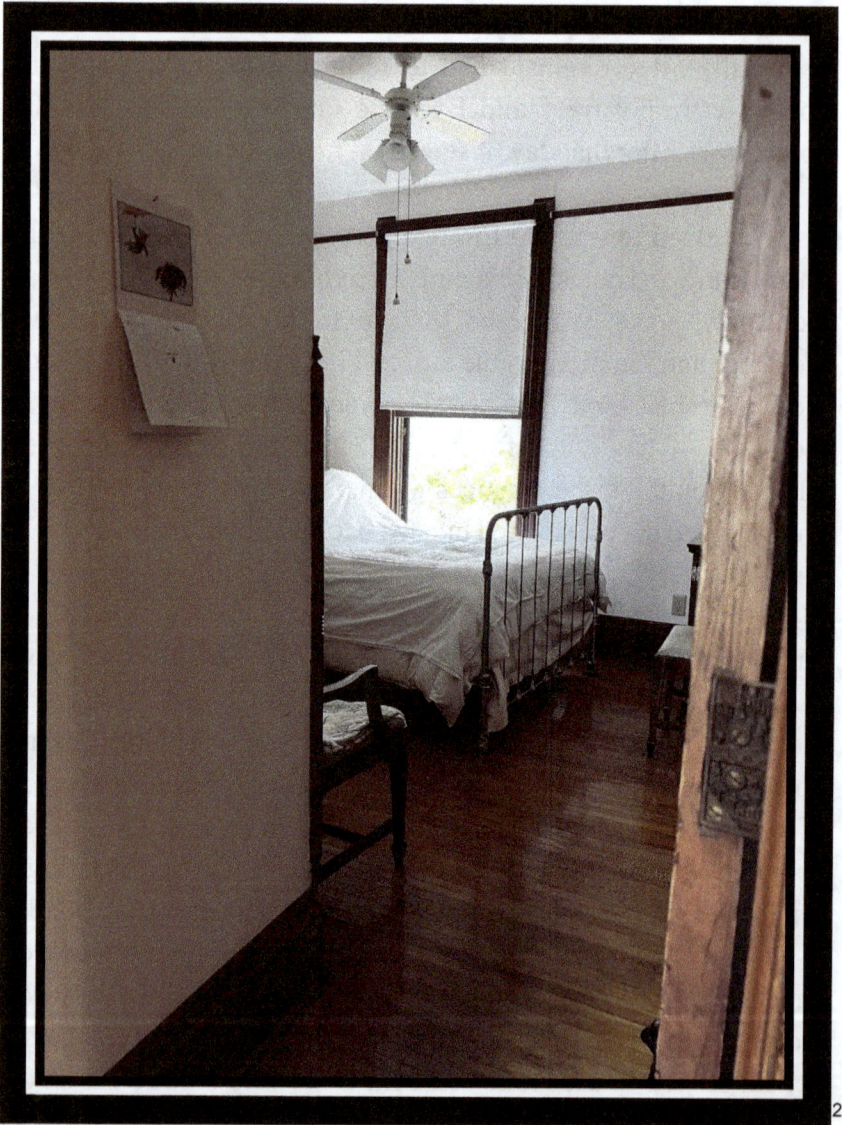

You exorcise people not closets, right?

Well, apparently there was something bizarre happening with the last owners in that bedroom closet, so they decided to have a priest come back to the home to bless that specific space. When they

---

[28] Bedroom at The Witch House. Photo: Josh Hughes

invited me back to do a Friday the 13th investigation, this bedroom was where I spent the majority of my time. It was the middle of the day and the Sprechers were outside doing yard work. I'm a firm believer that paranormal activity can happen either day or night, full moon or no moon. So this was the perfect time to take a visit and investigate the witch's house.

The energy was the same in this bedroom; heavy and unsettling. Right away as I was asking questions, I was getting knocks on the bedroom door and windows. I went through the names of the previous known inhabitants and received a knock in response twice when I asked if it was Charles. It was then when I decided to bring out the Ghost Radar. One of my all-time favorite devices that spirits can manipulate to provide you with one word at a time. This is where things got a little more bizarre. Through the ghost box, it knew I was sitting on the bed. The next two words that came through were "clothes" and "off." I'm not going to jump to conclusions on that one, but it was a good laugh when I shared it with the Sprechers.

The house on Rosemary Street is one of my favorite spots in Waukesha to visit when I jog because of the history that surrounds it. Right across the street we have the Ethnos Bible Institute, which used to be one of Waukesha's last springs-era resorts, in addition to a TB clinic and a veteran's hospital. It's not frequent that I see the Sprechers outside of the house, but when I do we share a few kind words and an update on how things are going. It's a privilege that I've been able to get to know more about the haunted history of this home and learn from the owners who have experienced the events themselves.

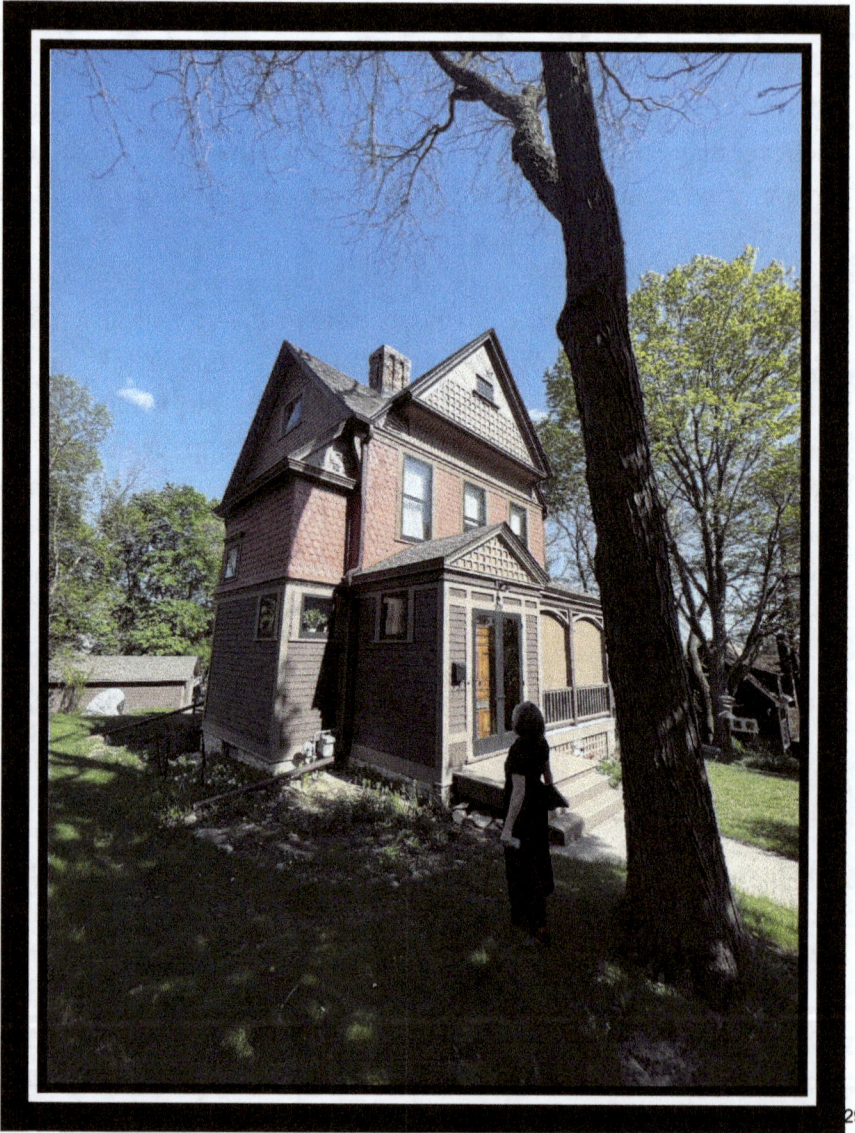

[29] The Rosemary Street "Witch House." Photo: Josh Hughes

76

EXORCISM IN WAUKESHA?

While St. Joseph's Church does not have its own exorcist, it was here that a scared family came after having strange experiences in a house they were renting in downtown Waukesha. It was the early 1970s and exorcism fever was sweeping the nation. After the scariest movie ever made was released, many people thought they too were experiencing something they would call demonic. The family that went to St. Joseph's seeking help didn't think this was the case at first, but eventually the priest that helped them made a wild proclamation that would change their lives forever.

Out of respect for the family involved, all names have been changed.

A 1974 article in the *Waukesha Freeman* tells the story of the DeLeon family who had four children and recently moved into a house that the wife's late uncle owned in 1967. Ever since the uncle passed, the house sat vacant - except for one month, when the former tenants moved out because they said they were experiencing ghosts. Something the DeLeon family laughed at, but shortly thereafter realized this was no laughing matter.

One of the first nights after moving in, the four-year-old daughter came to her parents and said in the middle of the night she saw a man standing by her bed. He proceeded to pat her on the head and then patted the heads of the siblings she shared the bedroom with. Like all good parents, they said it's just a bad dream and not to worry about it. But after more than one night of their four-year-old saying she saw the same thing, all the members of the family started to pay attention to the house a bit more. That's when they started hearing footsteps in the house when there was no one else around. Lights started turning on by themselves and phantom smells were abundant throughout the home.

One afternoon when the kids were at school, the mother invited over a cousin and shared a few of the bizarre incidents with them. Of course, this was silly to the cousin until the mother brought up the story of the man the four-year-old was seeing. When she mentioned the head patting, the cousin's mouth dropped. She had to remind the mother how their uncle used to pat them on the head when they went to bed. Exactly like this ghostly figure was doing. At this point the DeLeon family starts to believe that perhaps the uncle that had passed in the home might still be lingering around. Then one day while the children were in the basement, the daughter pointed to an old jacket that hung on the wall. She immediately said, "that's the jacket the man wears."

The husband still claimed that the footsteps were just sounds of the house "settling," but other noises continued like laughing, arguing, and strange voices. The wife claims that objects would sometimes be thrown down the stairs when there was no one else home. She also started getting dizzy spells when she went to church at St. Joseph's. In fact, during one mass the spells got so bad, almost to a migraine level, she fainted in the pew.

The wife eventually told the story to Father Richard Korzinek, a Catholic priest. When he was interviewed by the paper, he confirmed that she seemed to have some kind of claustrophobia when she went to mass. He became convinced that the house was haunted not by her uncle, but by a demonic force because "people who think they are hearing the dead speak actually are hearing a demon."

Father Korzinek said that someone in the house must have a connection to satanic activities, but the mother disagreed saying that her uncle was a devout Catholic who was not into any kind of occult practices. Nonetheless, Father Korzinek performed an informal exorcism of the house, using a fourth century prayer to try and cast the demon out. By the end of 1974, the priest thought that the evil spirit was no longer in the house, but the family disagreed. The teenage son said he still heard footsteps, the wife still heard sounds, and the four-year-old was still seeing this man in her bedroom at night.

Eventually the family did move from the home, but not until after years of enduring all this paranormal activity. Perhaps the exorcism was ineffective, or it simply didn't need an exorcism. One might hope that this was just the uncle interacting with his family in spirit. The love that one has for their home and their family is worth a few pats on the head as you slip away into a slumber.

[30] St. Joseph Church. Photo: Josh Hughes

CEMETERIES

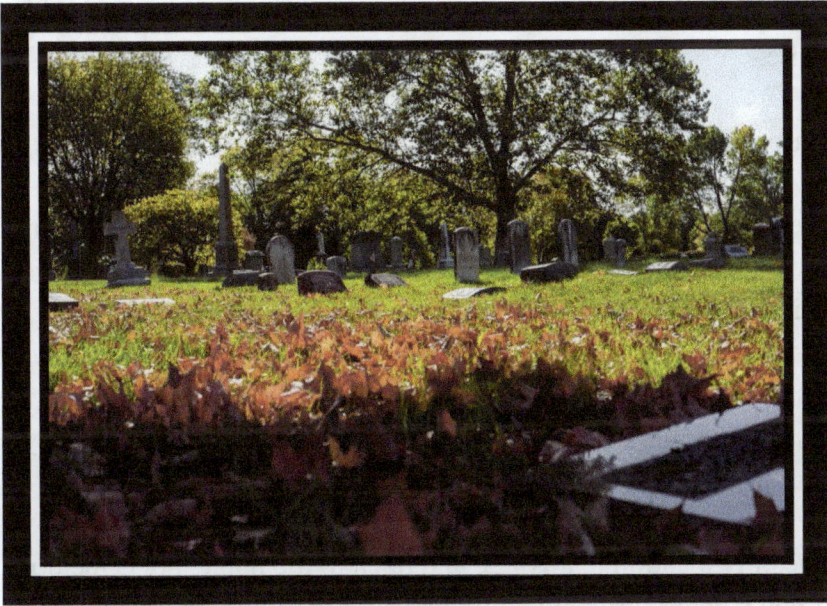

[31]

The summer of 2022 I was training for my seventh triathlon. When running, I seem to always have a destination in mind and this particular day it was Bethesda Park. As I took sips from the water fountain and stared at where the Dunbar Oak used to be, I got this overwhelming sense of urgency to jog up to Prairie Home Cemetery. It's not too far, what the heck. I could use some new photographs for the Waukesha Ghosts Instagram. I'd been there a number of times before and each time I sought out another grave associated with my stories. Today I was lucky enough to stumble upon the Hille family gravesite without much difficulty. As previously mentioned, there are a number of graves. I went to each one, snapping a few photos.

---

[31] Prairie Home Cemetery. Photo: Josh Hughes

As I knelt down to inspect the grave of William and Hulda, I was taken aback. I double checked the date on my phone and stared at the graves with my jaw nearly hitting the grass. Today was July 11th, the most tragic day on the farm when these two took their own lives. Whether it was an astonishing coincidence or a force that led me there that day, it's become one of my favorite personal stories to share.

Unfortunately, chances are you won't be as lucky as me to visit and investigate the many locations where these stories take place. I've been fortunate enough to visit the Hille farm, interview Anita, investigate the Witch House, tour the old Fox Head Brewery building, sit in the haunted basement of Club 400 on Friday the 13th, and the list really could go on and on. Most, if not all, are private residences or businesses that aren't going to open their doors for the general public. Club 400 might be the only outlier and they'll certainly welcome you in with open arms for a tour and a drink.

The only location that is free and open to the public are cemeteries. If you want to further explore these stories and more, you're in luck because Waukesha has quite a few cemeteries to visit.

The first reported cemetery was downtown Waukesha on Wisconsin Avenue between Grand Avenue and Broadway. Once the land for Prairie Home Cemetery was established, it is not known how many bodies were moved from this unknown location. Saint Joseph's Cemetery on East Broadway is where many of Waukesha's Catholic citizens are buried including my ancestors, the Price family. There is also a smaller cemetery that hasn't been used since 1951 called Northview Cemetery. The old poor house and asylum was eventually moved to the building where the Huber facility now is located. If you trample through the field behind the facility and make your way up the hill, you'll find a small collection of graves and memorial as well.

Not only do these cemeteries offer a quiet and respectful environment, you're about as close as can be to the people that experienced these events firsthand. Not to mention the beautiful masonry involved with old gravestones that seems to be a dying art in itself. I've spent a lot of time in these cemeteries and others across the world. If you're lucky, there might be something there that wants to interact with you. If you do choose to visit and try an investigation of your own, treat the property and gravestones with respect. Afterall, the bodies six feet under were living humans at one point like you and me. Treat them as such.

THE SUFFRAGIST AND THE SPECTER

Nestled within the quiet green of Theodora Youmans Park lies more than a tribute to a pioneering woman's legacy. It harbors a story that echoes with the eerie murmur of the past. While visitors today might know this park only as a peaceful public space named after one of Wisconsin's fiercest voices for women's rights, few suspect that the ground beneath them holds a ghost story tied directly to the shadows of both social progress and suspected murder.

Theodora Youmans was a cornerstone of Wisconsin's women's suffrage movement in the early 20th century, a time when the very idea of a woman casting a vote was met with ridicule and resistance. The term *suffrage* itself derives from Latin, *suffragium*, meaning "to vote." Despite modern confusion, it has nothing to do with the word *suffer*, though many women like Theodora endured their fair share of societal marginalization in a world that saw them as second-class citizens.

Though the word *suffragette* is often used today, it wasn't the term of choice in the United States at the time. In fact, it was considered dismissive. The "ette" suffix implies femininity but it is also a diminutive term, like calling someone "little." So, suffragette was a label American women rejected. The preferred word was *suffragist*, a more neutral term that reflected the seriousness of their cause. For anyone who believes political correctness began in the 1990s, history tells a different tale. It was already alive and well in the 1890s.

Every significant city had its women's clubs, spaces where women gathered to organize and strategize in pursuit of voting rights. Their activism helped shape the nation, but it also had complexities. Many of these same leaders, Theodora among them, were also proponents of the temperance movement, which eventually contributed to the rise of Prohibition, a legacy that history views with far more mixed feelings.

It is within this backdrop of activism and reform that a ghost story emerges, one recorded in the *St. Louis Post-Dispatch* in March of 1902. The article recounted a haunting that took place in Waukesha, inside one of its oldest homes. While the author declined to give the exact address, now a respectable and well-behaved house, it explained, it did hint that the property once belonged to the family of a well-known Waukesha club woman. At the time, the most prominent club woman in Waukesha was none other than Theodora Youmans. But curiously, the article never confirmed the woman's identity.

The story described a young girl, likely Theodora herself, who had just moved into the old house with her family. Exhausted from the day's labor, she drifted to sleep in her new room. But in the dead of night, she awoke to the presence of a man standing silently beside her bed. One hand hovered near her pillow, the other clutched a wooden stick. He had a long, unruly beard, and his eyes, she would later recall, were "terrible, cruel, and hard."

She ran to tell her mother, who dismissed it as a dream. "Stuff and nonsense," she called it. But the girl refused to sleep in that room again, at least not for several days. When she finally returned, so did the ghost. Her parents were jarred awake by a piercing scream. Rushing to her room, they found her unconscious. The paper described it as a "swoon." When she came to, she tearfully described seeing the terrifying man once again.

Not long afterward, the family sold the house. Its next owner, an older Waukesha woman, claimed to know the spirit's origin. According to her, a bearded man had lived in the house years prior. During that time, a wealthy cattle buyer had passed through Waukesha. With no inns yet established in the village, the traveler stayed as a guest in the bearded man's home.

It was a fatal decision.

The cattleman was never seen again.

The bearded host claimed the man had left early the next morning. But no one ever heard from the cattle buyer again. Whispers of murder circulated. The suspicion was heavy enough that the homeowner quickly sold the house and fled the country.

Whether justice was ever served is unclear. But the story does not end there.

When the house changed hands again, years later, a remodeling project unearthed a disturbing find. While digging in the cellar, workers reportedly discovered a number of human bones. The woman who had once experienced the hauntings, perhaps Theodora herself, believed that the spirit of the murderer was tied to the place of his crime. She theorized that the ghost continued to appear until the victim's body was found and the truth finally exposed.

Was it Theodora who saw the ghost of the long-bearded man? We may never know for certain. The article preserved her anonymity. But for a woman whose life was defined by the pursuit of justice, equality, and truth, perhaps that early brush with the supernatural fueled a deeper fire. A ghost that haunted not just her sleep, but maybe, in some small way, inspired her fight for a more just world.

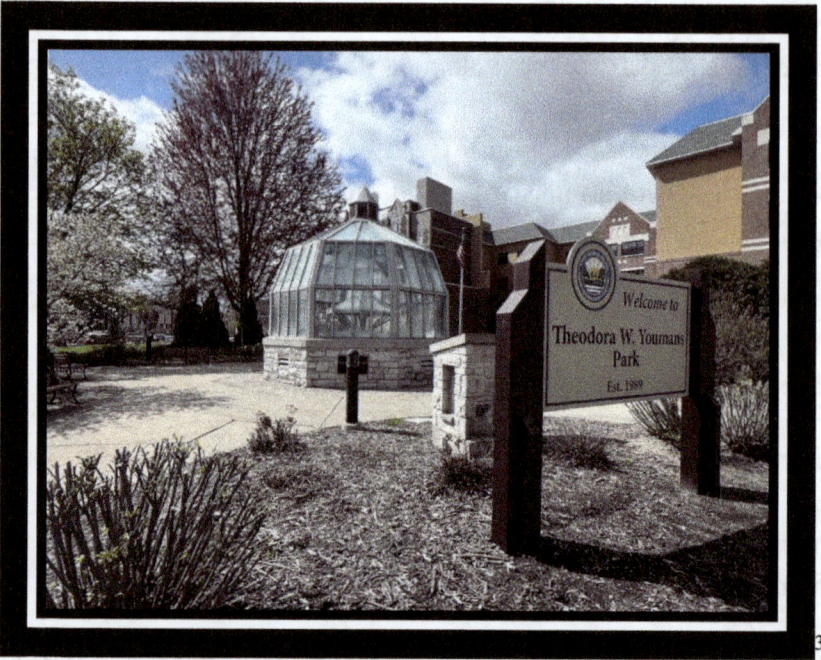

32

---

32 Theodora W. Youmans Park. Photo: Josh Hughes

88

THE GREEN LIGHT OF
ST. PAUL AVENUE

The roads that carve through Waukesha carry more than traffic and time. Some carry tragedy. Some carry memory. And some, according to the stories, carry something not entirely of this world.

St. Paul Avenue is one such road.

Running parallel to the modern highway that was once known as Highway 59, St. Paul Avenue leads us toward a modest bridge where Moreland Boulevard crosses the old road. Beneath that overpass lie the tracks of a railroad, and it is here, in the early 1930s, that a terrible accident occurred.

A car carrying four teenagers lost control and flipped near the railroad. The crash was devastating. One of the girls riding inside the vehicle was killed on impact. But her death became more than a simple roadside tragedy. According to long-circulated rumors, her body fell into the open car of a passing freight train. It was only discovered miles down the line. That mystery and horror left its mark on the area. And perhaps, something else remained behind.

Since then, those who pass by the bridge at night have sometimes witnessed something inexplicable. A strange green light, sometimes described as a haze or a glowing wisp, has been spotted drifting near the railroad and over the road. The sightings might have remained local lore if not for a chilling account printed in the *Milwaukee Journal* in 1984.

A local mechanic was driving home late one night when he encountered the phenomenon firsthand. He described seeing a green light, roughly the size of a stop sign, detach itself from the air and attach itself to his moving car. What happened next is difficult to explain. The car began to spin, as if directed by an invisible hand. The engine died. The battery was drained. The mechanic sat alone in the darkness, heart pounding, paralyzed with fear.

Eventually, the green light floated away. Just as suddenly as it had appeared, it was gone. And just like that, the mechanic's car returned to life. The engine started as though nothing had happened. But the man was never quite the same. He was convinced he had experienced something otherworldly.

The modern Highway 59 has since evolved, part of it now known as the Les Paul Parkway in honor of Waukesha's famous native son. But the ghosts haven't moved on. If anything, they've spread.

In 1965, *The Waukesha Freeman*, the city's trusted newspaper and one we'll return to later, reported a curious outbreak of ghost hunting. Bands of teenagers had begun gathering near another viaduct, one that crossed beneath the highway on the western edge of town. The cause of their fascination? A story that would soon sweep through the community.

A local high school student had been walking near the viaduct when he claimed to have seen something strange. Two disembodied heads emerged from the shadows, floated silently, then vanished behind a bush. The encounter rattled him. Word spread quickly. And soon, groups of up to forty students were sneaking out at night, forming ad hoc expeditions into the darkness to seek out the viaduct spirits for themselves.

They turned it into a kind of ritual. A ghost party. The kind of gathering where curiosity overpowers fear, and legend becomes a social event.

But it may have all started here, with a flipped car, a vanishing body, and a green light that does not behave like anything of this Earth.

For those who drive the Les Paul Parkway today, there is little to suggest the strange history that lingers just beneath their tires. But if you ever find yourself on St. Paul Avenue late at night, near the old bridge and the tracks that cut through the past, keep an eye on your rearview mirror.

Something may be following.

HALLOWEEN WITH THE
BAKER'S DOZEN

Maple Avenue, 1889

Everyone knows the date. October 31st. Halloween.

But few pause to ask why this particular night became associated with spirits, costumes, and all things eerie. To find the roots of the celebration, one must travel back thousands of years to the misty hills of the British Isles, where the ancient Celts marked the transition from fall to winter with a festival called Samhain.

Samhain was not merely the changing of the seasons. It was a sacred passage, a liminal time when the veil between the living and the dead thinned, and the spirits of the departed might roam freely across the earth. To protect themselves from these wandering souls, the Celts wore costumes and shared fortunes to predict what the new year, beginning November 1st, might bring.

As the Roman Empire expanded into Celtic lands, so too did Christianity. Church leaders co-opted the holiday, layering their own observances onto the ancient rites. They moved All Saints' Day to November 1st, and All Souls' Day to November 2nd, establishing a three-day religious observance known as Allhallowtide. During the Middle Ages, November 1st was known as Alholowmesse, or All Hallows' Mass. And thus, October 31st became All Hallows' Eve. Over the centuries, that name was shortened to the word we know today: Halloween.

This blend of ancient superstition and ecclesiastical tradition set the stage for countless ghostly encounters and mysterious happenings. One such story occurred in Waukesha, Wisconsin, in the year 1889.

At the time, a hotel known as the Morse House stood along Maple Avenue. Owned by William Morse, it was a stately establishment that often appeared in the social columns of local newspapers. His daughter, Carrie Morse, was a notable figure in Waukesha society. She was a founding member of an all-female social club known as the Baker's Dozen. The women gathered monthly for conversation, laughter, and community.

In October of 1889, their regular meeting took place at the Morse House. That year, their gathering fell on Halloween.

The *Waukesha Journal* reported on the party, describing a night filled with whimsy and charm. Each guest's plate was adorned with a tiny decorative cabbage, colored in black and yellow, the official colors of the Baker's Dozen. Hidden inside each cabbage was a fortune written in rhyme. They dined on chicken salad and sherbet, with the paper noting that the cooking was "past criticism." After the meal, the room was cleared for dancing.

But once the clock struck midnight, the night took a turn.

According to the newspaper, "the reign of witchcraft and the supernatural was ushered in." The women experimented with charms and spells, undoubtedly inspired by the spiritualist craze sweeping the nation during the late 19th century and Morris Pratt's Spiritualist "Temple of Science" built in nearby Whitewater only the year previous. Without warning, every gaslight in the building was mysteriously extinguished.

Then came the ghost.

The article described it as a "genuine, bona fide ghost," wrapped in a burial shroud. A skull was clearly visible at the top of the apparition, and its fleshless arms swayed as it glided through the darkened hallways. Its skeletal form was revealed in what the reporter called "the most appalling and hideous manner."

Terrified and unable to muster the courage to perform an exorcism, the Baker's Dozen scattered in fear. They hid from the figure, waiting in silence until the phantom vanished as suddenly as it had arrived. The party broke up in the small hours of the morning, shaken by their otherworldly visitor.

What exactly happened that Halloween night at the Morse House? Did the women conjure something they could not explain? Was it a prank, expertly executed during a time of heightened belief in the supernatural? Or did the Baker's Dozen accidentally summon a spirit from beyond the grave?

No photographs exist of the event. Ironically, Carrie Morse would later marry W.G. Mann, who would go on to become Waukesha's first well-known photographer. Had the haunting occurred just a few years later, we might have had an image to study.

Tragically, the Morse House would not survive into the next century. It was destroyed by arson in 1896. Since then, no similar spectral sightings have been reported on Maple Avenue. The ghost that stalked the halls that Halloween night appears to have vanished with the fire.

But the story remains. And for those who know where to look, so does the uneasy feeling that something happened there, something that even a century later still defies explanation.

33 The Mann House, still standing at the site of the former Morse House Hotel. Photo: Josh Hughes

MY GHOST STORY

There's absolutely no way I can write this book without diving into what made me want to write it. Without Waukesha, I might not have any interest in ghosts whatsoever. The experiences I had as a young child have led me on a lifelong journey to further explore and understand the paranormal. For me, it all started with sharing stories with kids in the neighborhood. One of the most famous tales was of demon dogs that lived in the Saratoga softball field concession stand. Try explaining that one to your parents. Another more believable one was lights turning on in a neighbor's house when nobody was home. For me, it was seeing an eight-foot-tall shadow creature I would years later find out is known as "The Hat Man."

I won't go into great detail about my experiences with my friends, but I remember the most confident of the group made all of us believe that if we had any deceased relatives, that's who was haunting your house. Now I know that wasn't true, but it did give me hope that when we die, that wasn't the end. From there I set out to conduct my research. I secretly looked through the card catalog at Saratoga Elementary to find one of the only books about ghosts. Reading it in the tucked away corner of the library, I quickly learned there were in fact many types of ghosts.

The TV shows of my childhood paired with what I was experiencing made me nothing short of terrified. This was the doom and gloom era when Linda Blair was hosting ghost TV shows that basically made it seem the scarier the haunted house, the better. I had multiple experiences at my house in Waukesha and even a few over the years as our family moved to Hartland. Was it just a kid with an overactive imagination, did something follow me, or was I simply someone that attracted spirits? Perhaps all three.

Eventually this passion for horror, ghosts, and anything weird would lead me to check out local spots featured in Chad Lewis' books. That's all we had in the early 2000s and it was exciting to share this different side of me with my friends. When I started attending UW-Oshkosh, ghost hunting was the last thing on my mind. As I started my sophomore year of college, my roommate and I realized we had very similar experiences growing up. It was also around this time that my favorite ghost show "Paranormal State" came out. It got us thinking that maybe we could form our own paranormal investigation team.

Just like that, the Oshkosh Paranormal Investigation Group was born. With a solid group of people with varying interests in this field, we met weekly to chat about investigations, share our ghost stories, and just enjoy being around a group of people with a different interest. We eventually got our first investigation at Elsing's Second Hand Shop in Stoughton, Wisconsin. What I experienced that night blew the top off what I previously had known about ghosts and ghost hunting. From our very first steps in the door, people were being touched, names were said, EVPs were collected, and an overall sense of fear spread across the group. I had never been in a more active environment that seemed to interact with us at our beck and call. The young group of investigators were so petrified that we slept in one aisle of the antique store together, wrapped up like terrified little burritos.

That group had the privilege of investigating Elsing's twice with equally impressive results the second time. We also got to the Belvoir Winery in Liberty, Missouri before many of the big name TV shows did and had far better results than we ever could have imagined. I graduated from UW-Oshkosh before many of my other group members and left the team in good hands. After a few years, the group dissolved and I can say that we were the first and only, as of now, paranormal research team at UW-Oshkosh.

To be frank, this passion of mine was put to rest for a few years. There was a lot of transition going on with moving back to Waukesha, new jobs, and a new relationship with my now-wife. But like all good things, it came back into my life at an interesting time. I was recently married and my wife and I were looking for our first house. We had been cast on the HGTV show *House Hunters* which included extensive interviews about our likes and dislikes. I casually

---

34 The Oshkosh Paranormal Investigation Group. Photo: Josh Hughes

mentioned I wanted an old house with lots of character and "if it looks haunted, I want to live there." We settled on a bungalow at the top of College Hill that was built in 1918.

It was the perfect home, but it wasn't haunted.

… or so we thought.

After about four years of living here, my wife and I started to notice a few strange things around the house. You would sense that someone was around and you'd see things out of the corner of your eye. The night we ripped up the carpet in the upstairs, you could clear as day hear someone walking around the old wood floors. So I started to research the history of the house and the people that built it and lived here. Low and behold I discovered a woman passed away in our home in the 1940s, which made all the odd things we were experiencing lately make sense. The more the renovations increased, so did the abnormal activity. In fact, as we finished a bathroom renovation I was awoken in the middle of the night by what I swear was an old woman walking around our new bathroom.

After enough experiences, I summoned the courage to call the second owner of the home who had done extensive renovations in the 1980s. Not only was I interested in all the work he had done, but I ended the phone call sheepishly asking which bedroom the old woman died in. There was a slight pause, followed by a chuckle. He said, "My wife told me not to tell you about that." Since I already knew there was a death in the home, I went on to explain that we had indeed noticed a few odd occurrences and were curious if they had as well. The previous owner went on to tell me that this woman had passed in one of the second story bedrooms. That room is now my office and was formerly a bedroom for their son. He would frequently say he saw an old woman in his room at night. There might have even been mention of this woman tucking the little boy into bed. The previous owner ended the call with, "What you have in your home is a very loving spirit that is looking after you and your family."

Well, doesn't that just put you at ease.

It was around this same time that my Dad sent me a photo from the bandstand at Cutler Park. In the background of a somewhat grainy photo taken by his co-worker, you can see the faint outline of a little girl in a Victorian era dress. I reached out to the Waukesha Ghost Walk Facebook page, included the photo, and received a response that was along the lines of "I have no idea what that is, but do you want to be a tour guide?" Mike Huberty was on the other line of communication and I met him a few months later to learn about the Waukesha ghost tour. After hearing about all the stories I am sharing with you today, it was game on. I was obsessed with all the bizarre history in my hometown and couldn't wait to rejuvenate a tour that had been dormant for a number of years.

When I was younger, hunting ghosts was all about the thrill of the hunt. I wanted to be the cool Bill Murray scientist type that is quick with a joke and always gets the girl. But it was just a hobby. It was something bizarre that I had a lot of experience in and knowledge of that made it just taboo enough for me to be interested. My college years taught me there were many people like me who wanted to explore this further. It introduced me to the technology of ghost hunting, cold-calling supposedly haunted houses, and the reality that many people were now introduced to this world through popular television shows.

While my interest level has varied over the years, I finally feel like I've found my niche that was meant just for me. As an expert of all things spooky in Waukesha, it's become a great honor that I can teach other people about these stories, develop theories, and make lasting friendships surrounded by our universal love of the macabre.

---

[35] Home circa 1920. Photo: Waukesha County Historical Society & Museum

CLOSING

For whatever reason you opened this book, I hope you learned something new about Waukesha. It's always a joy when I share these stories with someone who has lived their whole life here and didn't have a clue any of it happened. While my knowledge is well beyond my years, it didn't happen overnight. Long hours of scouring through historical documents and old newspapers has been a true passion of mine and I still shock myself how much I've retained over the years. But the journey doesn't stop here. While I know Waukesha might not be the first, or second for that matter, city you think of for a good old-fashioned ghost story, we've certainly had our fair share of odd, bizarre, and horrifying things that have taken place here. From mythical healing water to a cursed farm, a love triangle to a witches house that few dare to visit, this is the place I love and call home.

Whether you live in Waukesha, Oconomowoc, Austin, or Donegal, there are stories to explore. I'm always fascinated that people don't expect these sorts of events to have taken place in a relatively small city like Waukesha. That's what I love. It almost takes you off guard when you realize a love triangle put Waukesha on the map for a summer. You almost still don't believe it when there's a little boy in the cemetery and we don't know his true identity. That's when your curiosity gets the best of you and you have to find out more.

My efforts to make these stories as authentic as possible has introduced me to some wonderful people. Being able to experience these things for myself has made telling the stories that much more enjoyable. When I hear a story, I want to see it. When I see it, I want to touch it. The journey to know and experience is never over. Now that you're armed with this knowledge, I encourage you to seek out that ghost story you've always been curious about. Is there any truth to it? You have tremendous resources available at your fingertips, a library you can visit for free, and a historical society with volunteers that are just as curious as you are to learn more.

It's never fun to call this the end, because like death, it's only the beginning

ACKNOWLEDGMENTS

Ending this book I have to start at the beginning. First and foremost I have to thank my parents for never discouraging my interest in movies, TV, music, video games, and wanting to explore things that go bump in the night. Even when they might not have always understood what I was doing, there was always support.

The incredible group of friends I worked with at UW-Oshkosh made me realize that this was something that brought people together from all walks of life. The one thing we all had in common was ghosts and how we wanted to spend long nights investigating and even longer hours reviewing evidence.

Do you remember when you told your spouse you believe in ghosts? I don't but I'm sure it was early on in our relationship. To my wonderful wife, Allison, for always making sure I know she doesn't want me to bring that stuff home with me but wishing me good luck on my ghost hunt. You've never scoffed at me for spending long hours on my laptop and your excitement in reading the first draft made me realize I didn't need to throw my computer in the garbage.

None of this would exist without Mike Huberty and the wonderful American Ghost Walks team. If he hadn't answered a Facebook message about a ghost girl in Cutler Park, none of this would exist. You've always been there to help out with the Waukesha tour and beyond. The book probably wouldn't sound half as good without the dedicated copy editing of Anna Huffman. In addition to being a talented reader and artist, she's always on top of me to get my tour dates scheduled.

To the wonderful staff at the Waukesha County Historical Society & Museum, they always seem to know I'm up to something interesting and never bat an eye at an unusual research request. Their binder of newspaper clippings involving murders, ghosts, and anything unusual is the heart of this tour.

The extended American Ghost Walks family, KJ and Jeff, for always listening to my story ideas and investigating a couple spots with me in Waukesha and beyond.

Last but not least, this one is for Sam. The greatest writing partner I've ever had. While you didn't contribute to ideas, you listened without judgement. You never asked me to hurry up, unless you were hungry, and always served as inspiration even while you napped in my office chair. You were the greatest animal I've ever known and in death you're still showing me you're around. Goes to show ghosts aren't just for humans.

SOURCES

https://www.clubwaukesha.com/

archives.carrollu.edu

https://www.gmtoday.com/the_freeman/news/waukesha-cold-cases-who-
is-the-local-little-lord-fauntleroy/article_704f0e80-4d7d-5df0-
be74-c7b910f7587e.html?=/&subcategory=27%7COther

https://www.linkstothepast.com/waukesha/poorfarmwauk.php

The Life Story of Dr. David Roberts - page 41

Waukesha County Historical Society & Museum

Waukesha Public Library

ABOUT THE AUTHORS

Growing up in Waukesha, Josh Hughes has had interactions with the paranormal since a young age. In his time at UW-Oshkosh he met a group of like-minded individuals and was able to form the university's first-ever paranormal research team that has been to locations across the Midwest.

Mike Huberty is the owner of tour company, American Ghost Walks, preserving and boosting haunted history across the United States. In addition, he writes songs, plays bass and sings in Weird Wisconsin rock band, Sunspot.

www.ingramcontent.com/pod-product-compliance
Lightning Source LLC
LaVergne TN
LVHW022325080426
835508LV00013BA/1319